When Love Is Not Enough

When Love Is Not Enough

Bringing Spirituality and
Coping Back to Families and Homes

Dr. Thomas L. Page

iUniverse, Inc.
Bloomington

When Love Is Not Enough
Bringing Spirituality and Coping Back to Families and Homes

iUniverse books may be ordered through booksellers or by contacting:

iUniverse
1663 Liberty Drive
Bloomington, IN 47403
www.iuniverse.com
1-800-Authors (1-800-288-4677)

Because of the dynamic nature of the Internet, any web addresses or links contained in this book may have changed since publication and may no longer be valid. The views expressed in this work are solely those of the author and do not necessarily reflect the views of the publisher, and the publisher hereby disclaims any responsibility for them.

Any people depicted in stock imagery provided by Thinkstock are models, and such images are being used for illustrative purposes only.

Certain stock imagery © Thinkstock.

ISBN: 978-1-4620-1354-8 (sc)
ISBN: 978-1-4620-1355-5 (hc)
ISBN: 978-1-4620-1356-2 (e)

Library of Congress Control Number: 2011908516

Printed in the United States of America

iUniverse rev. date: 05/19/2011

"Faith First"

"Have faith in me, and you will have life giving water flowing from deep inside you, just as the scripture say…John 7:38"

TABLE OF CONTENTS

Special Dedications

To "Momma: Finally, a book that I am able to dedicate to you and say "thank you" for being the mother that I could be proud to say was the one who gave me the most challenges, but the most unconditional love in the world. I was never alone while you were on earth and I thank you for not leaving me alone in death…looking down on me from Heaven…Thank you.

To "Pop": My rock, my strength and the very first male who raised me with love, and raised me to be more than I wanted to be for myself. When you died in 2000, my world crumbled, but you continue to live in my heart and I managed to keep my promise to you. This book is dedicated to you in celebrating you home in Heaven, looking down, smiling, knowing that you are always in my heart and soul.

To Joanne VanLenten: Thank you for taking me in as a son through the years when a young man needed a support system. You gave me more than love. You showed me what it was to "be free" by living your life in faith, and trusting only in God. I will forever carry that with me…and practice what you taught me.

To William Peter Nelson Jr.: Thank you for being the best mentor, friend and "second father", and for being the person who looked at me and saw the best in me, and never stopped being there for me, supporting me on. You are truly my spiritual father, in every sense of the word. Thank you.

To Jeremiah (my grandson): I know you are too young to read this book now. But know that this book is also dedicated to you, in the hope that when you read this, you will know that you will always be guided by males who will love you, support you and guide you with love, encouragement and spirituality. Take that love, embrace it and know that this is your gift from God…to you. I love you "Boop Boop".

And to Dr. Jocelyn Sherman…my spiritual mentor and friend for life. Your spirituality and support through our journeys together gave me the inspiration for writing this book. Thank you. Thank you. Thank you.

HOW THIS ALL BEGAN

CHAPTER ONE

✏

"CHRISTINE"

Christine. There is so much that I can say about my mother, Christine. My mother is the very essence of who I am. My mother is the one of the very reasons that this book is being written. You will not find very many women like Christine today.

Momma (who I call Christine) is the reason why I believe in God and the true meaning of faith. I remember many mornings that I would get up and see momma looking out the window, listening and having her hand on the radio, crying, praying for her family, and especially her children. I remember one morning in particular, when I saw my mother in a different light. I was never the same after that. It was on February 13, 1972, the day after my brother died. That morning for some reason, I got up a little earlier than usual. I tiptoed out of my room like I usually did so that I wouldn't disturb momma from what I now know was "her time with God". As I was walking towards the room where she was at, I noticed that momma was crying and singing. This was something that I really never expected from my momma. I knew that my mother could sing. She would sing songs by Sam Cooke, Lightning Hopkins, and contemporary singers of her time. I never heard my momma sing gospel songs before. This was the first time in my life that I knew what "faith" actually was. She had her hand on the radio, listening to Rev. Ike, praying, and crying. You must understand that during that time, radio would have late night and early morning services on the radio. Momma never attended church because she felt because she couldn't read and she didn't want to be embarrassed. She would always tell us that she didn't have anything to wear. So, Rev. Ike would tell all the listening viewers to put their hand on the radio and he would pray for them. Momma would put her hand on the radio and just weep while Rev. Ike prayed. But this crying was not the ordinary type of crying my mother usually did. It was a cry of joy. It was the type of cry that gave a peace that passed all human understanding. In her crying, she kept saying, "My faith is enough to believe in you, Lord. You know what you are doing. You gave me my son and You took him away. I don't understand why, but you know what you are doing. I will trust in you, Lord." And then she would break out in song, " I will trust in the Lord. I will trust in the Lord. I will trust in the Lord til I die." I did not understand this. How could anyone, much less a grieving mother, trust in a God who took the life of her child, and still have the faith to stand upright and thankful. I realized that momma had that one thing that she taught all of us. Momma lived by it and died by it...spirituality. *When love was not enough...she prayed and trusted in her* **spirituality.**

My momma was a virtuous woman. My momma was the stay-at- home mother that made sure that pop had food ready when he got home from work. Momma made sure that all of our clothes were clean, we were fed well and our homework was done. She was the disciplinarian of the family. Momma did not know how to read or write efficiently, but was known for her "mother wit", common sense and a beautiful heart. Momma would always make sure any person that came into the house was welcomed and fed. The first thing that would come out of her mouth would probably be, "Are you hungry?", "Did you eat?". Momma always cooked with these big, huge pots and even though we were poor financially, momma made rice and black eyed peas seemed like a feast. I still remember the fish, cabbage and the skillet cornbread that momma made and it became my favorite. The last time momma made it, I literally cried because that was the meal that pop always liked and she cooked it when he died. I remember the love that went into cooking it. It was that type of love of a mother that made cooking and being in a family at the time memorable and one that everyone would remember…knowing that you are fed…knowing that you are taken care of…knowing that you are loved in this way.

Momma was not a very affectionate person…at least not physically. Momma was not a touchy, feely person unless she put her hands on you when disciplining you. Momma's love was also shown through her whippings. YES….I said whippings (beatings). Momma was the one person me, my brothers and sisters feared, especially if we did something wrong. "Pop" had to be the nurturing one. At times, I believed Pop was scared of momma and what she would do if we (or him) stepped out of line. Momma always believed that you were to do the right thing (no matter what) and if you didn't get what she was telling you through talking, she would show you even better. Momma was tough. Even if momma was wrong, it wasn't our place to tell her that she was wrong, or that she made a mistake. That was always reinforced by pop and between the two of them, there was an order of discipline and respect that was to be given to the two of them and any adult that walked in and out of our path. Momma did this to make sure that we knew that we could always depend upon the two of them, and to stay a child as long as we could. It was not our place to be grown…but to "grow" and grow like the mindset of

Jesus. I've always remembered 1 Corinthians 13: 11 and I've always kept that in my heart: "When I was a child, I talked like a child, I thought like a child, I reasoned like a child. When I became a man, I put childish ways behind me." Even Jesus grew up as a child. I guess mom knew what she was talking about so that when the time came for us to become adults, we would be well prepared and have the same respect and skills to raise our children. Momma protected us and kept us on the right track. She taught us right from wrong and instilled morals and values. I have always come to know that with momma….*when love was not enough, she **mentored** us.*

Momma will forever hold a special place in my heart because of what she did to keep us together as a family. She was the glue that kept us together and bonded us for life. She will forever be held in the highest esteem for doing what she needed to do to make sure that we did not need for anything. At times I would get so upset with her because there were times when with the little money she had, she would still give it away and sometimes left with nothing but her pride. But, momma didn't mind. She would rather see us happy or help someone else because that was momma. She always believed that God would always bless her and her family and come through whenever she needed Him. Family was very important to momma. She lived for her children and for that I am a better person in this world…for when love was not enough…she showed and gave me *insight.*

CHAPTER TWO

∽

"KAPERS SR."

Kapers Sr. (my pop) was the backbone and foundation of our family. Pop was the "silent warrior", the part of my life which taught me to live and live knowing that you did something good for someone else as well as for yourself. I will always remember when I was a child, I would always go with pop to work when we didn't have school or when he had to go to work on weekends. I would sit there and just watch him work. The one thing that made me a proud son was the fact that he took pride as he simonized cars and would make cars beautiful as they come off of the lot. He would take his time and put his heart and soul into his work. Just by looking at him, I could tell that loved what he did. He was the breadwinner even though momma took the check every week and balanced the budget. His heart was momma. Pop worshipped the ground that momma walked on. Momma could do no wrong according to the book of "Kapers". When momma would have her moments, all pop would do is just sit their patiently, quietly and without moving (as though he was the most content person in the world) When she would finish, he would say, " I love you, too, Christine". That would burn momma up even more, but that was their relationship. Pop would know exactly what momma wanted and needed. I remember going to the store with pop to get some food for momma. I would get a cabbage and he would reply, "that's not big or green enough.". I would get a small box of rice and he would reply, "That is not big enough". But, pop being pop, he would let me go ahead and get it. When I got home, it was as if pop spoke those same words (he told me in the store) into momma's mouth. I could not believe how in sync they were. Pop took good care of his family. Even though pop didn't get paid what he was worth, he made do and he always was a great provider. Between him and momma, the family always managed.

Pop never complained about how bad things were. Even when the both of us had to go back and forth to the VA hospital in East Orange, we would talk about everything, but he would just be as cool as a cucumber and took life as it came. As sick as pop was, he still managed to take care of his family. When pop had his leg removed due to diabetes, I can tell that it devastated him. It seemed as though it took the life right out of him. Pop was never the same after that, but his favorite statement of all to keep me from worrying about him was, "At least I am alive…and Christine is ok." There was always an unspoken bond between me and my pop. I would be his mouthpiece when he couldn't say what was on his heart. I felt his pain and I knew his heart. When pop passed away in December of 2000, I lost a big part of me that I never spoke of. What I felt, seemed to have went in the grave with my father. Two days before he died, he said to me, "Baby, I am ready to go home." I said, "Pop, you are going home tomorrow.". He responded and said, "No, Baby…I am ready to go home". I knew what pop was talking about and all I can say was "I know, Pop". He made me promise him that I would take care of momma if anything should happen to him. Once I made that promise, pop was at peace. He really never spoke after that. He would just stare into space. When I would go to the house in those final days, I would go in there and just sit with him and I told him that I would take care of things. I knew the time was soon coming and I saw tears come to the side of his face. That was when I had to face reality that I had to now be the pillar he wanted me to be. Pop died the next day. I knew when he died. No one had to tell me. I felt a soft warm breeze on the back of my neck and I stood up. I called the house and I was told that they were taking pop to the hospital because he stopped breathing. They revived him once more, but I knew it was the end of pop's life here on earth. Pop was a man that I will cherish forever, love and remember as a family man and a man who was dedicated and loving to his family and especially his wife, Christine. When love was not enough…pop showed and gave **allegiance**. I miss "Pop" kissing me on top of my forehead when I was a child. I miss him speaking gibberish just to get a reaction from momma. I miss the days taking pop to the VA hospital and having that bonding time with him. I miss "Pop". Pop is the other reason why this book is being written.

CHAPTER THREE

~

"THAT WAS THEN"

Throughout most of my life, I have been blessed with a two parent household, brothers and sisters and a life that I really enjoyed and appreciated. People may not believe it …but it was fun sometimes being poor. We got a chance to appreciate each other. We were forced to do without and be content without it. When we did have enough money, momma and pop made sure we did things together like going to the drive-in theaters, Carvel and/or Guernsey Crest Ice Cream and going to Brooklyn to spend time with my mom's sister, Aunt Josie Mae. It wasn't about the money. It was about spending time as a family and making sure that we supported each other and was there for each other.

Having a two parent household took a lot of the burden off of one person and gave the assurance that if you were not loved by one, you were loved by the other. During those growing times, we would observe our parents on how they reacted to things and did things on a daily basis. We would watch TV and from watching television, there would always be this upstanding superhero that we all wanted to imitate and be like. I always wanted to be "Superman" because I wanted to be faster than a speeding bullet and I wanted to fly and swoop down and catch the bad guys. Thanks to my brother, I am still alive. I tried to play "Superman" and flew off of the top bunk of the bed with a towel tied around my neck and aiming toward the window. I went through the sheet of glass and thankfully my brother caught me…towel first. I ended up getting stitches and a good beating that I'd never forgotten. I learned not to play "Superman" anymore, but I did learn the value of family and that we learn from observation, imitation and modeling. We learned that we had to be careful because environment also played a role in how people respond behaviorally in specific situations and scenarios. Family as the foundation kept most of us stable in a world that was becoming unstable.

As a doctor and professor, I come to find that my parents did exactly what theorists have been telling us to do for years. Let's get to the basic ideas first. It was the role of family and the home environment that was to prepare us as children and to focus on the appropriate behavioral skills in a family and social setting. As we were growing into our adolescent (teen) years, we started learning from other people. Our parents were still that basic and firm foundation for us, but we now learned to observe outside of our family realm, into unchartered territory called an environment, imitating and modeling those we now wanted to become, still keeping our values and morals intact.

As far as operant conditioning, there was no such a thing as paying children to complete required chores and school work which was what momma used to call "your job as a child". There were only rewards for getting "A's" on your report card, rites of passages (birthdays, teeth coming out, etc.), or excelling in a sport or competition in an achievement made outside of the normal everyday activity.

"THAT WAS THEN"…

CHAPTER FOUR

⟋⟍

"THIS IS NOW"

Today, it seems that parents are learning from their children, instead of children learning from their parents. It seems as though that the roles have reversed. The behavior that children and adolescents possess today is not just something that has come out of the blue. This has been an ongoing plight to gain our children's respect. The thought of being their "friend" instead of their parents have given children and adolescents mixed signals, which is confusing them more each day. Parents have also allowed the fear of their children's aggression to succumb to their negative behavior learned. So instead of standing up to their children and being the head of the households, the parents "give in" to their behaviors and demands.

As a doctor in the field of Human Services, specializing in the field of Counseling Studies, I have studied (and still studying) the behaviors of children, adolescents and adults to come up with some sort of explanation why things have taken a turn for the worse when it comes to our families and the future of our children. I know that many parents may not want to hear this, but I can promise you that what I am about to tell you will be an eye opener and one piece of advice that I have found to be crucial in my family's life and has made a change in how we live and grow and connect even closer as a family. In a research that I have done with adolescents and families, it has come to my attention that if we don't come back to the basics of "family" and "spirituality", the streets will take over our children and adolescents, and parents will be left holding the bag of shame and guilt because of familial practices that we chose to neglect and overlook.

Young adult urban males across the United States are often absent from the conversations regarding that which addresses the integration of their expected values and norms of acceptance with that of one's belief relative to their spirituality. In studies that I have completed within the past few years, African-American young adult males were found to show no organized system in place to mark their Christian beliefs and spirituality. Such an outcome suggests such views have created in some individuals an increase in their self-destructive behavior. With such results as these, there is now a growing awareness and concern about such loss in faith among African-American adult males and families across the United States. Sometimes we forget that the strength of any family lies upon the head of the household...the male. Women have become disgusted and frustrated, having to take up the slack for what has become the roles they now have to play as head of the household because of the roles that they have let men surrender as a way of giving up and throwing in the towel because the relationship "doesn't work". However, we cannot fold up, nor can we succumb to excuses and frustrations because things did not work between the mother and father. There is one factor that remains unchartered by males and females alike who are breaking up families and not facing the facts that they base their lives on sex, money and "what we can do for each other"…there is spirituality and what we can do to find it , get it back and bring our families back together.

Most parents never make it mandatory or see it important to wake up on Sundays to go to worship service. Children (and especially) adolescents now have a choice as to if they want to get up on Sunday morning or stay in bed. The biggest obstacle facing the parents I deal with on a daily basis is that " I don't want to deal with the hassle of fighting with them to do something that they do not want to do." So the parents ignore the facts that their children are not being "spiritually fed", but being strengthened by "facebook", "my space", "twitter" and "technology". It is funny to me that we can get our children up for school, and fight them tooth and nail and nearly threaten them to get up and go to school so that they can get an education. We, ourselves, as parents, literally break our backs trying to get up each day and go to work, because we know that if we don't work, we don't eat. We can't buy and do for our families the way that we should. But guess what, parents, if your children are not being spiritually fed and you have given them that choice, you probably are not being spiritually fed. This weakens the family structure and causes the foundation of any and all relationships to deteriorate (crumble), including the lives of our children.

Now for the wake-up call. How is it that we can get up in the morning, open our eyes, plant our feet on the floor, start our day, take care of our children, and survive from moment to moment without thinking of how this is possible? Who gave us our limbs and our life to have a family in the first place? How did we get this far in life to say that we have done this on our own? Surely, I hope that you are not thinking that we just came through our mothers and we are surviving on just our looks and our chances. There is a factor that we are forgetting here. We are not here by chance and there is a higher being that keeps us going each day. Sometimes, it bothers me to know that this spirituality that we possess is not nurtured, practiced and taken seriously as we do with making our children go to school and forcing ourselves to go to work. I keep thinking about Tina Turner and how she took a song and made it a national anthem to those who no longer see love as a factor in relationships. Tina Turner had a point..."What's love got to do with it?" My point is, "When love is not enough…try faith…try allegiance…try mentoring… try insight…try living (life coaching)…try yielding. But if you want to get to the heart of getting your life back in order along with your family…try going back to the basics…spirituality.

CHAPTER FIVE

"THE IMPACT OF SPIRITUALITY"

Despite such awareness, we are just touching the surface focusing directly on the impact of spirituality based on Christianity in the lives of urban young males and families in the United States. One of the biggest concerns that faces me in trying to help create balance in the lives of African-American families (as well as all families who struggles with this issue) is to get parents to see how some of their young African-American young adult males make sense of their Christian spirituality when dealing with those factors creating the social breakdown of the family structure and to one's own community when such is not part of their psychosocial development as spiritual beings...especially without the support and training from their parents. For some of you who may be reading this book, a light may have just come on and reality has come to light? How can we as parents, let something of such importance, slip away from us and how could we have dropped the ball on this issue?

There are the assumptions among a lot of the parents that I have interviewed who have raised their African-American young sons in their Christian faith and hence provided guidance in their decision making and values through spiritual and community activities and practices seem to no longer exist in a world where Christian spirituality now has a different meaning, especially in the lives of young adult males. That is why I did the research and completed this book, to provide a framework that illustrates how family, church, and the community in part (together) can help young African-American young adult males and their families in the community cope with their feelings of alienation and develop more self-reliance, while avoiding problems, and seeking Christian spiritual support from others, bringing it back to the families and the homes.

HOW DO AFRICAN-AMERICAN YOUNG ADULT MALES PERCEIVE SPIRITUALITY?

The African-American young adult in the urban community does not internalize Christian spirituality, but instead utilizes observable behavior, rather than thoughts, feelings and motivations, which may be viewed as a private and personal experience. Christian spirituality is something taken to be true without proof by a deeply personal and unique experience of finding new purpose and meaning in life. I believe that spirituality is a process through which people seek to focus on what matters most, building lives on eternal truths, and becoming what GOD (and not what we think) created one to be. African-American young adult males have tried multiple methods by which to cope in their families and communities to meet their interpersonal and community needs. I believe that Benson (2005) stated it better, and I concur that the "self absorption of young males enables them to bypass the confusion and pain of trying to give their emotions some coherence; it also helps them avoid the realities of being flawed, vulnerable, ordinary human beings. African-American young adult males may find it difficult to identify a spiritual experience, to express themselves and to find a spiritual base to receive personal growth.

CHAPTER SIX:

"THE ONE THING PARENTS MAY NOT WANT TO HEAR"

The question of why so many of our children and young adults (especially males) in the United States have not developed adequate coping skills highlights the role of others in helping the youths, such as the parents, the community, the parents, the church, the parents and the school. See, I told you that this is something parents may not want to hear. But, keep reading and stay with me here. The families struggling the most financially and spiritually are those of the African-American community where male roles are absent from the lives of the African-American young adult males in the urban community. The lack of paternal presence leaves these young adult males to discern (decide for themselves) individually the needs that must be built in to "grow into adulthood" on their own. It is not their fault. Again, I must say that this is not their fault.

Most (if not all) males are judged as to their worth or value in the context of father's absence. Impaired contact or lack of contact with a father appears to have its most dramatic effects on African-American male young adults. African-American young adult males have been affected by its economic and social dislocations experienced within the urban communities, and are encompassed (contained) by the street life, and the devastation of the drug trade, drug and gang wars, and the war on gangs and drugs. I have worked in law enforcement for 13 years where I have witnessed these African-American young adult males witness their fathers, brothers, and peers being incarcerated. I am not letting these young adult males off the hook, nor am I defending their actions for their present behavior, but as parents, you must realize that the urban communities have been affected by the post-industrial decline in job opportunities, therefore leaving working-class and impoverished urban communities to suffer more. With the rate of our young African- American young adult males dropping out of school at such an early age, becoming fathers at an even earlier age, and these type of life experiences with drugs and gangs (defending and dying for territory that even isn't ours), African-American young adult males in the urban community are challenged as to how others (society, etc.) view them and what people do not understand about them and their experience.

THIS ISN'T JUST AN AFRICAN-AMERICAN THING...

The integration of Christian spirituality as a coping strategy has been particularly difficult for some citizens in the United States society. The reason I write about the African-American young adult males and their families is because I am a proud African-American male from the urban community. I live there and will probably always live there. This is where I was raised up, trained and brought up by my parents. This is also where my work and ministry begins and end. In my community alone, in the city of Paterson (New

Jersey), the death of African-American young adult males seems to keep climbing. The death of our young people through violence, gangs, and drugs are staggering. But we must not forget...again, this is not so much the fault of our young adult males, but the lack of instruction and training that has been given to them to keep them on the right path. The responsibility will eventually fall on their shoulders, but without the support and guidance from family, community, schools and the churches, the killings will continue. The senseless deaths will continue.

Through my research, I have observed young African-American males and their families having difficulty talking about, experiencing and identifying with a Christian spiritual base and value system which has historically been a source of coping for the majority of members of the African-American community across the United States. Yet, there is an absence of information regarding spirituality and its role in particular for those young adult African Americans and families regarding their social and emotional functioning as accepted citizens in the United States. Therefore, I explored the lived experiences of several African American young adult males using Christian spiritual beliefs and values as part of their coping strategy to offset their social and emotional functioning as successful citizens in the United States society.

After receiving my PhD, I continued my study on spirituality and coping of the African-American young adult males and their families. I needed to analyze and evaluate the lived experiences of those young African-American young adult males using Christian beliefs and values as part of their coping strategy in the hopes that we can get families to fully understand the importance of being connected, going back to the basics, and offsetting their social and emotional functioning as successful citizens and males.

CHAPTER SEVEN

❧

"THIS IS HOW IT WORKS"

The world perspective of the African-American community is grounded in a strong Christian spiritual belief system. This particular spiritual belief system links the cultural beliefs and practices of the African-Americans to effective coping strategies that result in positive outcomes in situations of risk and adversity (bad fortune). Spiritual coping of the African-American community represents the degree to which beliefs about GOD are used in managing adversity (bad fortune), enhancing resilience (the ability to recover) by providing a basis for optimism and the ability to recover from adversity (bad fortune). By not developing the relational skills needed to face significant risk and adversity (bad fortune) in the urban community, African-American young adult males' coping skills have been compromised (bargained with). In order for us to get back to the basics and bring spirituality and coping back to families and homes, I will demonstrate how African-Americans young adult males may be able to utilize spirituality's support system in and from the community to strengthened coping skills.

IT IS NEVER TOO LATE...

Within the development of the African-American community, the integration (building in) of Christian spirituality can foster forgiveness which necessitates a focus in the urban community as a way of surviving the experience of living in poverty, chronic unemployment, high rates of incarceration, homelessness, high crime neighborhoods and fewer financial resources. The integration (building in) of Christian spirituality in the African-American community can also foster hope to African-American young adult males and their families who suffer from low self-esteem, poorer physical and mental health and decreasing quality of life.

SO WHERE DO WE BEGIN TO PICK UP THE PIECES YOU MIGHT ASK...

Let's start from where we are right now. Yes, we are in a messed up situation and it seems as though it is not fixable. Yes, it is going to be hard to get this family back together because too much has been broken in order to fix it. But it can be done. It will be done. All we have to do is get started from where we are right now and begin picking up the pieces. Let's get started.

"THE STARTING POINT...FROM WHERE YOU ARE"

The one main question that you need to ask yourself as a family, and as a family with a young African-American male (or it can be any family with a young adult male): "What role has Christian spirituality played in defining the coping skills needed in the life of young African-American males in the urban community?" I believe that for many of us the answer is simple. Many families have not gone through any type of spiritual with their children, much less your young adult son.

Now as I have stated earlier, most African-American young adult males are suffering with the alienation from fathers who were physically and emotionally distant, with the lack of ability to feel, a loss of male energy, and a crisis in male identity. Within the urban community, the plight of the black male is evidenced through homelessness, committing or being a victim of violent crimes, and using illicit drugs. Additional evidence can also be seen through dysfunctional and non-traditional families, the absence of male bonding, juvenile delinquency, unemployment and poverty.

The integration (building in) of Christian spiritual coping provided by families, church and community of those young adult males who do believe and practice spirituality represents the degree to which beliefs about GOD or a HIGHER POWER are used in managing adversity (bad fortune), providing a basis for optimism and the ability to recover from adversity (bad fortune). Coping for the African-American young adult male in the urban community can be a group centered strategy whereby these particular young adult males rely on their family and social networks for managing risk and adversity (bad fortune).

In part of my study, I'd completed several life coaching sessions with a group of young adult-males (all of different ages, races and cultures). In this session, a few things came to light that all of these young adult males had in common. None of these young men ever dealt with spirituality and they all suffered from stress. The stress that these young men were dealing with was hardly the stress I dealt with when I was growing up. If technology has a downfall to it, you are witnessing it as you are reading. The use of technology now has young men in trouble and even imprisoned. These sights provide anything from dates to porn sites that are of easy access to our children and young adults. The young men attending the sessions dealt with the stress of the following: Early fatherhood, STD's, gang violence, being bullied, verbal abuse, dating abuse, physical abuse, sexual abuse, unemployment, sexual identities and just being themselves. In these sessions, I have come to realize and confirm that the stress of males in general and found mechanisms of masculinity that accompany these young adult male gender roles often resulted in emotional stress. These mechanisms included: the emphasis on prevailing (at any give time) in situations that require fitness and strength; being perceived (aware of) as emotional and therefore feminine; the need to feel powerful in regard to sexual matters and work and; the need to repress (hold back) tender emotions such as showing emotions that are restricted according to traditional masculine customs.

As far as coping goes, these young adult males had different standards by which to estimate stressful situations and coping within this particular group which was affected by their perception of spirituality…at least at first. Once I dealt with them on another level, spirituality became a valuable option for most of them. One of the biggest disappointments that came up in this session was that in dealing with them in talking about family, the parent(s) placed greater emphasis on the religiousness, spirituality and conformity (if any) on the females instead of the males. Yes, this is true. We must not really be surprised at this.

As a life coach, I have come up with many strategies to help these young adult males grasp the concept of spirituality and how to take the approach. I had to be real with these young men just like I am going to be real with you, the reader.

LET'S HAVE A REALITY CHECK AT THIS POINT…

I am sure that parents and those helping children and young adults may not want to hear about this first step I am about to give you, but it is a reality check, it is real, and it must be mentioned and adhered to if you want family success and success of your young adult male. If you really want to start to bridge that gap in developing Christian spirituality practices in the lives of African-American young adult males (and all young adult males suffering from lack of spirituality), we can start through with the involvement with the church and community. That's right. I said it...the church and community could foster (promote) involvement; providing mentors for the African-American community and the community at large; providing mentors for the African- American young adult male in the urban community; helping African-American young adult males to develop self-regulatory (governmental) abilities; fostering identity development; providing a supportive and stable community and offering a relationship with a powerful and loving other.

I have been in church all of my life and if it wasn't for Pastor Tony VanZanten and the support of the Madison Avenue Christian Reformed Church, I can't really say that I would be writing this book today. Being in church provided all of us young people who attended the church at that time (Voices of God /Teen-Time) a frame for identity.

I AM NOT SAYING "GO AND JOIN A CHURCH"...

I am saying, or shall I say for a lack of a better term, "recommending" that if African-American young adult males and their families in the urban community are willing to negotiate life and comes to grip within the context (pattern) of Christian spirituality and the church rather than participate in a gang, they have a better chance of avoiding prison, creating early pregnancy, and the numerous other negative outcomes that limit their ability to achieve health and happiness. Also, notice that I said, "and their families". The African-American young adult males should never stand alone in this struggle. This is not just their battle. It is our battle...a community battle...a church battle...and mostly, a family battle.

The study that I completed was an attempt to research the rationale of the various components (elements) that can contribute to the integration (building in) of Christian spirituality in the African-American young adult male in the urban community based on the following assumptions that resulted from my research:

- *African-American young adult males suffer from a lack of appropriate male models in the urban community and they have few-African-American men role models with whom to bond.*

I thank God for men like my pop, Pastor Tony VanZanten (my spiritual mentor and my second dad), Rev. Jerry Zandstra, Art Gardner, Elias Lumpkins, William Peter Nelson, Jr., Willie Siebles, Rev. Louis Richardson, William Gilmore, David VanLenten and many more who were key figures in my walk through life. These men molded me into the person I am today. There were many more men in my life, but these men stayed with me from a child, through my adolescent years, and helped me make decisions through my college years and gave me a benchmark as to the man I became through their modeling and mentoring. I cannot thank these men enough for guiding me through a path that kept me safe. The men in my life came with no conditions. They came into my life with no expectations other than to be the best that I can be. The only thing that was ever asked of me was that I stayed in school and let me teach you and show you how to be a responsible, loving, caring and spiritual man, so that you can spread that same love and mentorship to other young men whose paths you will cross in your adult journey.

There were no rocket science methods in keeping males in the past together and in order. The community of men that surrounded me were also the same men who whipped (yes, I said "whipped") my tail when I got out of line, gave me great encouragement and praised me for the work that I'd accomplished and completed, ripped my butt apart and yelled at me when I did something stupid without thinking through the process, and always looked out for me and talked me through life's journeys. They didn't have to be with me. I always knew where they were and all I had to do was call them, go to their homes, or just reach out to them. But the things that I remembered most about these men were the fact that they prayed with me. They took me to church with them (and in some cases, attended church with me). They were not scared to show their feelings or emotions. Of course, these strong spiritual men did not wear their heart on their sleeves, but I could always guarantee that whenever I looked up to these leaders in my community, they showed their love, their tears and demonstrated through their love how proud they were of what me and other young males in my community did to make them and our community proud.

I think of the 4th Ward, where I was raised and I think about another group men who were in my community who did not go to church, but hung out on the corners. Yes, I remember those who would beat the hell out of us if they caught us smoking, drinking, or doing anything that we weren't supposed to do (even though they did it themselves). Their philosophy (thinking) was simple..."You do as I say and not as I do". Now, I am sure that you are thinking to yourself, how and why I would mention these men on the corners of my street where I lived. Why these men? These men also played a part in my life and taught me about the "streets." These men made sure that young children like me at the time were protected from all hurt, harm and danger. If they really saw that you had the potential to be somebody and they thought that you could make something out of yourself (which they saw in me), there wasn't a chance in hell that you were going to be on the corner or on any other corner. They all knew momma and pop. Momma and pop were the good Samaritans of our block and would raise most of these men. I am thankful for my brothers Terone, Kapers Jr. and Gordon, who really looked out for me (even when they didn't want to). I thank God for Be-Bop, Ike, Curtis, Cape Cod, Raymond and those brothers who were my extended family and helped me to be the person I am today.

You see, it took a special type of man back in the day to make sure that many of us young, African-American males did the "right thing". You didn't have to be a rocket scientist, or a person with a degree. These men had heart, a love and passion to bond with young brothers like us, to keep them off of the street, gave time and time again, making sure that we knew they were "present" and would be there for us whenever we needed them…" But if you messed up.. that was you're a—". I never suffered from a lack of appropriate male models in the 4th Ward urban area. I had many African-American, White and Hispanic men role models with whom to bond with and for that I want to thank all of these men (and the many male role models not mentioned) for taking the chance at raising me… *For when love was not enough…there was male bonding.*

CHAPTER EIGHT

～

"A REALITY CHECK"

What I am about to share with you are some points that I hope will help you to understand the struggle of African-American adolescents and young adult males. This information also will pertain to every adolescent and young adult male in the world. We may be divided by ethnicity, but we are bound together by gender and the struggles they all face as growing, young men.

- *The self-esteem of African-American young adult males in the urban community suffers from the pervasive negative images of blacks on the street, in schools and the media.*

Even though life has not worn me down yet and I am still looking somewhat young for my age, I must say that even in the midst of trying times, I did not have the technology and the easy access to the things that young adult males (and females) have in their possession today. We also did not have the mouths and the attitudes that most young people have towards their mothers, fathers, and adults in this present time.

"IT'S NOT THE FAULT OF THE AFRICAN-AMERICAN YOUNG ADULT MALE...AT LEAST NOT MOST OF IT..."

Let's do a quick reality check here. Sometimes we are quick to forget that these young adult males did not just come out of their mother's womb with the intent to cuss, fight and become violent. Remember that a child is trained and taught many of the mannerisms and behaviors that they have possessed. Without a male role in the contemporary lives of these young adult males, without the support from the family, churches, and community, these individuals actively practice a behavior until it becomes ingrained (firmly established) in their memory. Once this behavior becomes firmly established in their memory, they begin to arouse to that action and begin to repeat or call on that behavior in making decisions. If a behavior is to change, especially in the lives of the African-American young adult males, these young men must have and get the opportunity to practice it. Let me say that one more time for those who are reading too fast...

"IF A BEHAVIOR IS TO CHANGE, ESPECIALLY IN THE LIVES OF THE AFRICAN-AMERICAN YOUNG ADULT MALES, THESE YOUNG MEN MUST HAVE AND GET THE OPPORTUNITY TO PRACTICE IT..."

"LET'S FIRST SEE WHAT THESE YOUNG ADULT MALES ARE UP AGAINST AND GO FROM THERE..."

"NEGATIVE IMAGES OF BLACKS ON THE STREETS"

Now what I am about to say may have you thinking that I am going to be a little out there on left field and ignorant for making the following comment, but who cares…it's real and it's a fact. As much as we talk about gang activity and gang violence, I have to tell you that I thank God for some of these gangs. Notice, I said some of these gangs. I am not trying to defend them, nor am I trying to highlight them and making them out to be something that they are not. Some of these gangs are teaching these young adult males survival and teaching them the things that the parents, schools, church, and community dropped the ball on and should have been teaching them. I have a lot of great friends who are in gangs. When I worked in the jail, I developed a great rapport (relationship) with a lot of brothers whom I have great respect for. I don't respect them for the fact that they are in gangs. I respect them for rallying around and taking in that African-American young adult male who went astray and decided to take on a personal battle of wanting to be independent without the knowledge, know-how and the tools to do it with. They showed them love and gave them the financial support, the discipline to look out for each other and to make sure that no one in their circle stood alone. This sounds like something families are responsible in doing. This was their family. I remember when gangs became popular (at least in Paterson). It didn't start out about territory that wasn't ours. It started out as a community function in order to help the community build and protect their own through rallying together and making things better in their community. That was the purpose at first. As time went on…things changed. People changed. Times changed. Economics changed. Families changed. The spiritual make-up of the families changed. Something was lost and someone had to pay the price for it…our

African-American young adult males and all young adult males and females and children. So, even though the gangs still exist and still do what families supposed to do…

"THERE IS A BIG DIFFERENCE BETWEEN THE LOVE OF FAMILIES AND GANGS"

My friends who are still in the gangs (and whom I will always love and see as my brothers for teaching and loving me unconditionally) explained to me that if they had the chance to do it all over again, they would do everything in their power to make things right and stay the hell away from the gang mentality. I was taught that they (the gangs) will win you over with what you don't have and make sure that every one of your needs was met. This is true. It was also true that they would look out for you and make sure that you never stood alone in the circle of brotherhood. All of this true. But, the thing that made the difference in all of this was that all of that love and support came with a price. This price came with the allegiance that you had to make with your life, pledging only to them. It came with a price that could end up losing your life for it.

"IT'S NOT THE FAULT OF THE GANGS THAT OUR AFRICAN-AMERICAN YOUNG ADULT MALES (AND FEMALES) FLOCK TO THEM"

We let society tell us so many times that being poor was a sign of failure and weakness. We let society dictate to us that without money, we would be unsuccessful. We have been brainwashed to believe that the love of money is more powerful and more useful than the love of family. We have been told through the power of media and the movies that "Greed is good", and "the only way to have power over yourself and your finances is to "take it". So, if mom and dad didn't give it to us, and there was someone who could give that power and money to us, and would pay attention to us at the same time, why not go there. The gangs made sure they had the resources and during that time in the young adult males' life who was struggling, the perception was that the gangs had that power society was talking about. They had that greed and hunger for taking what they perceived was theirs. This looked good to those young African-American young adult males who didn't have anything except for the clothes on their back. How could we as a people and a community let society dictate such a life for our children. Taking it even further how could we as parents let it get this far that our children would have to go to such lengths when they could have gotten this unconditional love and support from home. It wasn't always about the money and the power. It was about being there; being present in your child and young adult's life.

We even let society tell us (as parents) that it is alright for our children to sleep in on a Sunday to recover from the hangover on Saturday to get the rest you need to start back to work on Monday. This is the same society that has given us a church, a liquor store and a bodega on each block, giving our children the choice between a good time of drinking or a good time of fellowship with the Lord.

"PARENTS...YOU ARE FAR FROM BEING EXCLUDED FROM THIS "BLAME GAME"..."

Parents...Many parents have become their children's friend. Since when does confusion like this happen? In many of my life coaching sessions, many individuals suffer from the heartbreak of their children confronting them and cussing them out because of the fact that they are just trying to be their friend. I'm sorry, parents.

If God wanted you to be their friend, he would have put you in another body at another day in time closer to the age of your son or daughter.

"YOU ARE NOT YOUR CHILD'S FRIEND...YOU ARE THEIR PARENTS."

Our adolescent and young adult males (and females) don't want you as a friend. They need parents. They need someone to teach them right from wrong. Our children need someone to spend quality time with them and let them know how beautiful they are, even when they are at their worst. Our children need to wake up on the holy day (whichever day you serve your God or Supreme Being) with you and serve together in the celebration of life...demonstrating unity as a family and being blessed that all of you are still together as a family, safe and secure with the God (Supreme Being) who made us. You need to sit down with your young people and turn off the television, shut down the computer, leave all phones and gadgets in your rooms and have a talk with each other. Yes, with each other. One of the most damaging things that we do to our children, especially adolescent and young adult is assume that they are responsible now and grown when you haven't taught them the true value of family, adulthood, and what it is to be spiritual and a person that they can be proud of. If you don't start taking back the responsibility and start taking back what God has given you as a gift...someone else will do the job for you...and you may not like the end results.

- *The self-esteem of the African-American young adult males in the urban community suffers from the pervasive negative images of blacks on the street, in schools, and the media.*

We have already touched on the fact about the negative images of blacks on the street, but how does this type of image play out for an African-American young adult male in the schools and the media? For many of us who are parents of African-American males and have went through the process, you already know how this scenario is going to play out. For those who do not have children and are thinking about the possibility, then this book is definitely going to enlighten you on what you need to do and watch out for in order for your future generation of African-American young adult males to succeed.

CHAPTER NINE

~

"SCHOOLS AND THE MEDIA"

When writing this book, I was contemplating whether or not to separate these two entities (things). I decided not to for various reasons. I know that I will be stepping on a lot of peoples' toes and even though I will not call any people out, the sting of what I am about to tell you will either leave a bitter taste of guilt in your mouth, or give you an eyesore full of self-serving intentions and greed, showing you the results of what you have destroyed in the process from this greed and guilt and self-serving intentions.... *the death of our young people.* Either way, our families, and our children end up lost...at least for now.

Our African-American young adult males already have to deal with a lot of issues in this world. This is a fact. During the development of the adolescent stage, these young males are dealing with social, psychological, cognitive and physical issues. These potential young men are really starting to become adjusted to their body image. This body image includes their weight and body and the onset of puberty.

There are other social changes during this adolescent stage that will begin a journey of increased awareness among male's body image and concerns about weight and muscular definition.

Self-esteem begins with the thought of one's body image and how they look and are perceived by others. You will see that as you read on, this issue of self-esteem will lead to depression and other factors of mental health issues that plague our African-American young adults today.

"NOW LET'S GET TO THE HEART OF THE ISSUE WITH SELF-ESTEEM AND OUR AFRICAN-AMERICAN YOUNG ADULT MALES..."

It is my opinion and my personal belief that society is not kind to the adolescent and young adult males, especially the African-American young adult males. Society has seemed to have put a label on this particular group, which find themselves asking questions as to "Who am I?", Why am I different from everyone else?, "What kind of person am I?", "Why doesn't anyone care about me and how I feel?", and "Why am I singled out?" There are many more questions like this going through the minds of the African-American young adult males, but these are specific questions that shed light on how and why others may make a judgment as to their desirability, their worth and their value. The media has portrayed most of the young African-American young adult males as "thugs", "hoods", "the lost generation", and my least particular favorite..."future incarcerated inmates". The media seems to have built certain models and images of the young African-American male in the movies as drug dealers, gang bangers, rapists, vicious attackers and criminals.

In the little television that I do watch, I am turned off by the fact that the only positive images that are portrayed on television are those of white, preppy groups of teens and adults that are always connected by love, and friendship. If you happen to see an African-American male in any type of television show, they are usually the sidekick of one of the white actors and they are usually the character portrayed as the fat brother that eats everything in sight, the jokester that needs to make everyone life and always the life of the party, or the brother that everyone is scared to talk to because of the thug image that he portrays. I thank God for Tyler Perry and his quest to make sure that there's a platform for African-American males and young adult males to be seen in a positive role. I am convinced that pretty soon, there will be a movie or show which will portray a young African-American male not always being a comedian, but bringing light to the issues that matter the most in the lives of young African-American adult males and the plight of family reunification. Everything does not have to be a joke about the way young African-American males live, nor do we have to settle to be the brunt of someone else's joke when it comes to the image of the way African-American young adults are perceived (baggy pants, white t-shirts, icy whites and colorful boxers).

Because of my conviction to help right a wrong that has been done to our young African-American males, it is my desire to help bring light to better explain how we might have come to this assumption of how we perceive African-American young adult males and help them redirect society's image of what they can and will be...successful. I would like to start this development by introducing you to a concept of thinking that I learned while studying for my PhD with Capella University. The concept (idea) is social learning theory. I became very interested and vested in learning about social learning theory to help me to understand a lot about myself, and how I can use this particular theory into better understanding the African-American young adults in my community and the community at large. When studying this theory, my intention was to write a book as to how this theory can be applied in explaining the African-American young adult male....how they got to where they are and how we can get them back to where they need to be..."*back to families and homes*".

When a person learns from observation (noticing and watching others), taking what they have observed and then imitating what they have observed, that process would be part of what the academia world would called *social learning*. We do this every day. Sometimes we are totally oblivious (not aware) of it. I did not really become aware of this concept (idea), or didn't get that there was a specific name for this learning principle until I actually studied the works of Albert Bandura. Albert Bandura (1977) suggested that vicarious reinforcement is a concept that means observing another person's behavior and reinforcing that behavior, therefore affecting the behavior of the observer.

WOW...DOES THIS SOUND FAMILIAR OR DOES THIS RING A BELL?

You may be wondering where I am going with this. Well, follow me and I will take you where I am going. It is important to understand that the African-American young adult male's behavior seems to have changed in the eyes of society. I would describe these changes as a sign of the times. This would appear to me to be a timely issue because of the dangers facing contemporary African-American young adults. The concept (idea) of just young adult males and females, in general, being "at-risk" describes an age following vulnerable to many negative forces in their developmental movement towards adulthood. Now, unlike their ancestors, who suffered more frequently from untreated and untreatable disease, today's African-American young adult male risk harm primarily from social illnesses. These social illnesses include: family, school, and peer groups. Now, just in case you didn't get that;

THESE SOCIAL ILLNESSES INCLUDE "FAMILY", "SCHOOL" AND "PEER GROUPS".

So, when your child is looking at their next television show, or you tell them to go watch television or get on that video game because you are too busy as the role of the parent to take time with them, or your adolescent (teen-ager) gets on that computer without your knowledge of what website they are on, just know that this is one of the falling social illnesses that plague our adolescent and young adult world. I can guess and make a fair assumption (something taken to be true without proof) that many parents don't even know that their child, especially adolescent and young adults males are being picked on, bullied, and forced to do things at school without your knowledge. Add to the fact that we have issues at home where children and adolescents are usually the targets misplaced anger, the fact that these issues not being dealt with, play out further and effect the young person's world through their school environment and social world that they deal with on a daily basis. Looking back, now, I can see that those little talks with momma and pop did me some good. Those talks were like a security blanket for me, knowing that they cared enough to become interested in the lies I told before momma whipped my butt…or even when momma would beat us first, then talked to us when she got a note from the teacher about our behavior at school. Momma and pop would take the time to make sure we understood what we were getting in trouble for, family for me. That kept me on the straight and narrow. *For when love was not enough…there was communication.*

CHAPTER TEN

◠

"FIVE"

N ow that you have this concept (idea) in your head, I would like for you to do this exercise with your Child (adolescent and young adult):

Throughout the course of the day, take the time to communicate with your children (adolescents and young adults) face to face. Just to be clear; do not do it via, text, phone, skype, facebook, or email. Make sure that you have physical face to face contact with your loved one.

Throughout the day you should have asked the following questions:

- How was your day at school? (at work…if it is the young adult)
- What did you do at school today?
- What worked for you today?

- What didn't work for you today?
- If you could start the day all over again…what would you do different?

I call these questions the "Family FIVE" questions because each of these questions are significant in making sure that the communication with your children, adolescents and young adults are being enforced throughout the day and this gives you the chance to get to know more about your child (adolescent and/or young adult), what they are doing and giving them the indication (sign) that your interest is totally into them and you care enough to value what they are telling you in conversation. If you notice the above title "Family FIVE", the word "FIVE is capitalized for a reason. As parents, guardians, mentors and leaders it can be very frustrating to talk with your child and only get one word answers. When this happens, we get aggravated and sometimes argumentative with our children (adolescents and/or young adults) because your interpretation of their communication with you may come across as "short", "not being interested" or "just not caring". The word "FIVE " is an acronym for:

F – FOCUS
I – INVEST
V-VERBALIZE (VOCALIZE)
E – EXPECT

FOCUS: When you "focus" on your child (adolescent and/or young adult), make sure that everything part of your body is focused in the direction of the child (adolescent and/or young adult). Make sure that you do not have anything in your possession such as a cell phone, or anything that would distract you from giving your child (adolescent and/or young adult) that time and attention.

INVEST: Invest the time with your child (adolescent and/or young adult). The more time you invest with them, the more that they retain and develop that social learning skill from you. Children (adolescent and/or young adult) will always remember the times you spend with them. In the time that you do spend with them, they will observe you. They will pick up certain meaningful body movements that will take the place of words in communicating a thought or feeling. At the same time, you will also reciprocate (return) the gesture by getting to know what they are feeling through their gestures and bodily movements.

VERBALIZE (VOCALIZE): Communication is a two-way street. Both must be able to put words together to create a sentence that make sense to each other. Now, this is where the hard part may come in. Parents, when you ask the five questions to which I have already offered you, here are some tips that will help you connect with your child (adolescent and/or young adult) and get them to create a dialogue (conversation) with you. **DO NOT ACCEPT "I DON'T KNOW", "OK", "GOOD", "BAD" OR "I DON'T WANT TO TALK ABOUT IT" FOR AN ANSWER.** These are easy, simple answers that children (adolescents and young adults) give to parents to get them off of their backs. If you see where your child (adolescent and/or young adult) don't have an answer for you at that moment, remember you have throughout the day and you give them this response: **"I WILL GET BACK TO YOU LATER FOR AN ANSWER"** Now, you have them at a position where they now have to give you dialogue (conversation) sometime throughout the day, making the connection happen and developing a social learning skill that they can practice and hone (master) going into adulthood. Just one more thing that you must remember parents, guardians, mentors, and leaders…If you do give them the latter response (I will get back to you later), you must make sure that you are responsible and do your part...**MAKE SURE THAT YOU GET BACK TO THEM BEFORE THE DAY IS DONE.**

EXPECT: Expect nothing less but their best when it comes to giving honest, truthful responses. Make sure you also respond with clear, honest and truthful responses. The expectation is to help the chid (adolescent and/or young adult) develop their social learning skills and make the effort to keeping it in the family. It is so easy to just say to your child (adolescent and/or young adult), "Well if you don't know or don't care, I don't either." This is where the breakdown begins and this is where we need to catch it...starting with the family. *For when love is not enough...try communication. For when love is not enough...try expectations.*

As a qualitative researcher, I must use a theoretical lens (perspective) to guide my studies, seminars and life coaching sessions and raise such questions such as of gender (for which my study are young adult males), class (urban poor), and race (or some combination) to get a full understanding of what I am about to address. The next concept that I would like to bring to light in redirecting society's image of the African-American young adult male and bringing spirituality and coping back to families and homes is that of *resilience*.

Resilience can be defined as good outcomes in spite of serious threat to adjustments and/or growth. Two conditions are necessary for identifying resilience. These two conditions are the presence of a significant threat or exposure to adversity and a determination that a positive adjustment has occurred in the face of misfortune. In the condition of the presence of a significant threat, this can mean the significant threat dealing with poverty, parental history of mental illness, community violence (to give a few examples). In the condition of exposure to adversity, examples would be that of:

the death of a parent or a victim of a crime. Threats to growth and exposure to misfortunes establishes risk factors. These risk factors have found to bring together in one's mind or imagination poor social, psychological and health outcomes. Risk factors can occur and have an increasing effect in building up the chances for poor outcomes opposite to those risk factors are protective factors or assets, which ease positive adjustments in the face of threat and exposure to misfortune. Traditionally, preventive factors have included family level (family functioning) and extra-familial (general social support) level.

NOW FROM ALL OF THIS INFORMATION GIVEN, THIS IS WHAT I KNOW...

The worldview of African-Americans is grounded in a strong spiritual/religious belief system, extended family and fictive kinship bonds, a collective social orientation, and affective expressiveness. Without these worldviews from the African-American culture, the social illnesses that African-American young adults suffer from will follow them through their adulthood. My completed research has linked the cultural beliefs, behaviors and practices of African-Americans to effective coping strategies that could result in positive adaptive outcomes in situations of risks and misfortune. Various spiritual coping mechanisms that helped in grounding a strong spiritual belief system in the African-American culture included prayer, contact with church leadership and members, meditation, religious television and music.

CHAPTER ELEVEN

ᵔᵔ

"WHAT I DISCOVERED"

***NOW THROUGH MY COMPLETED RESEARCH,
THIS IS WHAT I DISCOVERED...***

The spiritual coping mechanism that protected and grounded our fathers, mothers and forefathers and mothers before them are becoming non-existent. I remember a time when all of our families took the time to pray. I remember momma always praying. I truly believe that momma was the reason many of us lived as long as we did because if it was left up to most of us, we would not be around to tell anything. The song was so powerful in church that whenever we sang this song, I would visualize momma:

> *My mother prayed for me*
> *Had me on her mind*
> *She took the time and prayed for me*
> *I'm so glad she prayed*

Each and everyday
She took the time and prayed for me

When momma prayed, or even better yet, when all mothers prayed in the past, you knew they were praying ...and praying for all of us. When momma prayed, you knew you were protected under God's care. With her prayers, it made the world seem alright.

WHERE ARE THOSE PRAYING MOTHERS TODAY...? WHY AREN'T WE FEELING THOSE PRAYERS LIKE WE DID WITH THOSE "MOMMA'S" OF THE PAST?"

As far as church leadership, the churches seem to think at times that they can give outreach to the community from the pews where they sit on Sundays, instead of actually going out and doing the real outreach ministry, trying to actually reach out to the adolescents and young adults who has given up on family, the church, and God (Supreme Being) and made the streets their safe haven. I appreciate and love my pastor because he lives what he preaches. Pastor John makes us accountable as a congregation by making us get up out of our pews and actually walking the neighborhoods, praying and singing in the streets, walking for a cause to save our young people and bringing them and their families home (to the church). He is the example of a martyr going into the heart of the urban area where a youth has been shot and killed, meeting with the families and praying on the corner where the young adult male was killed. He brings attention to issues that matter...like taking the guns off the street, making it a safe haven for children, adolescents, young adults and families.

The churches also seem to teach "the family that prays together stays together" ...and that forgiveness and making statements like "things will get better if we just believe" will make all the difference in the life of our young people. Now, the problem that I have with that comment will be put in the form of three questions:

IF YOU BELIEVE THAT THE FAMILY THAT PRAYS TOGETHER STAYS TOGETHER...WHY AREN'T OUR FAMILIES PRAYING WITH THEIR YOUNG PEOPLE?

WHY ARE WE GIVING ADOLESCENTS AND YOUNG ADULTS A CHOICE IN THE MATTER OF WHETHER TO GO TO CHURCH (OR NOT)?

WHY AREN'T PARENTS TAKING A STAND, GETTING UP THEMSELVES WITH THEIR CHILDREN, ADOLESCENTS AND YOUNG ADULTS AND SHARING THIS SPIRITUAL EXPERIENCE WITH THEM?

I have discovered that spirituality can serve as a coping mechanism for African-American young adult males in the urban community contributing to a positive understanding of their adaptation (adjustment) or development. I found that, among young adults, the integration (unification) of spirituality promotes personal well being and lessens negative behaviors and outcomes. African-American young adult males who hear, and presumably internalize messages about spirituality tend to engage in greater level of anger control and fewer acts of overt aggression than their counterparts. I have discovered that the integration of spirituality plays a role in young adults' efforts to achieve emotional and behavioral self-regulation, particularly in times of personal conflict. Now just so that you are clear, and just in case you don't get anything else out of this book, get this point that needs to be repeated:

"ADOLESCENTS AND YOUNG ADULTS (NOT JUST THE AFRICAN-AMERICAN MALES) WHO HEAR, AND PRESUMABLY INTERNALIZE MESSAGES ABOUT SPIRITUALITY TEND TO ENGAGE IN GREATER LEVEL OF ANGER CONTROL AND FEWER ACTS OF OVERT AGGRESSION..."

NOW WHAT PARENT WOULDN'T WANT THAT??????

Now here is the most crucial bit of information that I would like to bring home to all who are reading this because no one is excluded when it comes to our adolescents and young adults.

Children's, adolescent's and young adult's development of spirituality is based on **observational behavior**, *rather than thoughts, feelings, and motivations.*

Now being that this book is about adolescents and young adults, I would like for the parents and adults to get involved. If you have children, then you should do this exercise. If you don't have children, consider yourself also being watched. You are also observed by them. So let's do this.

Think about what you did and said the last few days. Now for those who have adolescents and young adults, this is important because the one question that we seem to ask them when they do or say something that is not what you *think* you would do or say in your home is "Where (or who) did you learn that from?" I am going to ask that you list at least three thing s that you might have said or done that your adolescents or young adults might have *observed* and heard you say or do probably without you knowing. Think hard. I am sure that you can come up with something?

1. _____

_____

_____

2. _____

_____

_____

3. _____

_____

_____

Now that you have done that, take a few days and observe to see if your adolescent or young adults would say or do anything that was on your list that you wrote out. If you have at least one item that matches, this should give you an indication that if they can follow you in the negative items we talked about, imagine the power you can have by demonstrating to them the power of spirituality and using that as a coping mechanism. Let's not forget where we came from. For the urban community where I live (and probably where you live), the church is one of the primary institutional foundations of the African-American community. The Christian spiritual thinking in early childhood lacks a sufficient depth for the understanding and effectiveness of spirituality based on Christianity. Therefore, the understanding and effectiveness of the integration of spirituality must be learned during the adolescent and young adult development stages. It is the role of parents to make this happen. You can make the difference in the life of the African-American young adult male, but we may have to undo some of the damage that has been done to our African-American young adult males.

"AND WHAT DAMAGE IS THAT?", YOU MAY BE ASKING...
Well, let me break this down for you. You may be surprised at what you will read...or you may not. Either way...*IT'S REALITY. For when love is not enough...there is the truth.*

When it comes to the *spirituality in the lives of the African-American young adult males,* considerably less attention has been paid to associations between spirituality and well being prior to adulthood. There is the possibility that, as children moved into adolescence, African-American parents, families, and communities were particularly insistent that girls and young women be involved in the church. It was equally plausible that churches provided activities that were more appealing to and more fulfilling for young women than young men.

There can be a simple distinction between younger female adolescents (between the ages of 13-15 years) which exhibits more positive attitudes to Christian spiritual practice and affiliation than do the males. This can be explained by *socialization.* Among young adults, the differences relate more to gender orientation than to just maleness. Males who value the traits and characteristics often associated with the feminine are more positive about spirituality based on Christianity than males who do not value these so-called "feminine traits". The thrust of becoming non-existent in their Christian spirituality as urban young adult males from the church may not be a model characteristic of individuals who emphasize the personality characteristics of masculinity at the expense of the personality characteristics of femininity. Let's face it. We think of the terms used such as gentleness, healing, reconciliation, affection, childlike to describe the qualities of Christ; therefore to describe the ideal Christian disciple. Yet in society, generally, these qualities are more readily associated with the feminine rather than with the masculine. One can definitely come to the conclusion that the development of spirituality is negated through social expectations of male and femaleness.

HOW ABOUT ANOTHER REALITY...

How about *the environmental breakdown of the family structure and community?* In 2006, seventy-five percent (75%) of all African American school dropouts (and young adults of color) in their early twenties were under the supervision of the criminal justice system. I was one year into my research and this piece of news bothered me immensely while working in the criminal justice system at the time. I suppose that the average dysfunctional, poorly educated and violent young adult between 12-15 years old who is convicted of a crime and sentenced to ten years in an adult prison have as their role model an older, more sophisticated convicted criminal to help him develop during his formative years. Then he is released back into the community, in his early twenties, at his peak of his physical power, un-socialized, undereducated, and unemployable. This young adult male will be a model of the very person society wish to avoid.

I guess you do not have to question why so many young adult males are in this type of situation. We all know the answer. This type of situation place responsibility upon a number of factors: **the parents, the community, the church and the school (and not necessarily in that order).**

IT IS NOW 2011...AND WE ARE STILL REPEATING THIS SCENARIO FROM 2006. THE ONLY DIFFERENCE IS THAT THERE IS AN INCREASE IN AFRICAN- AMERICAN YOUNG ADULT MALES WHEN IT COMES TO

INCARCERATION AND EVEN A HIGHER PERCENTAGE WHEN IT COMES TO RECIDIVISM.

Let's now start making sense of this and see what we can do to reconnect with all of our adolescent and young adult males, especially the African-American young adult males in the urban community. This is enough reality for me …at least for right now. I am a product of the urban area. I am proud to be a from the urban area. My best childhood memories were from the heart of Governor Street, 12th Avenue and East 18th Street. I am proud to be a part of a rebuilding in progress. Rebuilding and reshaping our young adult males…. bringing them back to family and bringing them back home. *For when love is not enough…there are solutions.*

Now, what we are dealing with is simple to figure out. The problem for young adult males is that nothing is really 'whole' for them. Families are struggling and male role models are absent from most of their lives, leaving them to figure out for themselves what it takes to "grow into adulthood". Males are assessed (judged) in the context of a father's absence. Just in case you missed this point…

"MALES ARE ASSESSED (JUDGED) IN THE CONTEXT OF A FATHER'S ABSENCE…"

Impaired contact or lack of contact with appears to have its most dramatic effect on male young adults. Educators, mental health professionals and religious and community leaders struggle to find solutions to the problems facing today's African-American adolescent and young adult males (and other males of color) – high homicides, suicide, dropout and unemployment rates as well as increased drug use and disproportionate involvement with the criminal justice system.

The urban male young adults seem to be raising themselves and teaching themselves the art of self-preservation. Many parents have become physically excluded themselves from the inner lives of their children. Please, don't misinterpret this thought. For some parents, this was not intentional and having been a single parent myself, the scenario and the lack of support of a one parent household versus the two parent household forces our hands to do what we must do to survive…and the save the family we have left.

BUT KNOW THAT IS NOT AN EXCUSE FOR BEING PRESENT…

It is the contemporary "modern family" life, which leaves parents too busy to give an emotionally, invested presence in the internal landscape of a child's world (much less an adolescent of young adult male). With the many obstacles that today's parents try to maneuver and balance, key elements of raising urban young adult males are being overlooked. Because of the lack of male representation as the head of the household and family structure, most of the responsibility falls upon the single mother or guardian taking care of the young adult male. This becomes a problem for many female householders. Because there is no time for parents to connect with their sons, many urban young males take it upon themselves to set their own standards of discipline, creating their own self-image of what constitutes a young man, setting the stage for at-risk behaviors. This is a key piece of information and this is a big piece of the puzzle that must be solved:

"BECAUSE THERE IS NOT TIME FOR PARENTS TO CONNECT WITH THEIR SONS, MANY URBAN YOUNG MALES TAKE IT UPON THEMSELVES TO SET THEIR OWN STANDARDS OF DISCIPLINE,

CREATING THEIR OWN SELF-IMAGE OF WHAT CONSTITUTES A YOUNG MAN, SETTING THE STAGE FOR AT-RISK BEHAVIORS..."
"For when love is not enough...there is time."

HOW ABOUT THE MEDIA...

While those active parents are doing everything they can to make ends meet, their children, especially adolescents and young adult males are surfing down a slope of media consciousness, which stimulates them more every day. The media has appeared to set a standard for the urban young adult male as well as the standard for all young adult adolescents. The new standard consists of :

Sexual Encounters
Impulsiveness
Emotional Flatness
Isolation

The debate on the nature of masculinity is ongoing and continues to be a driving force for manhood acceptance when it comes to urban young adult males. Urban young adult males who had been sexually experienced reported a strong belief that sexual intercourse validates masculinity and increases closeness to a female. African-American males and males living in the urban areas were somewhat more likely than those of other racial/ethnic groups or residents of non-urban areas to have had two or more sexual partners. When controlling for race/ethnicity, urban males were significantly more likely than suburban males to have had multiple sex partners.

SO NOW THAT YOU KNOW WHAT YOU DIDN'T KNOW...WHERE DO WE GO FROM HERE?

"POSSIBLE SOLUTIONS TO BEGIN THE PROCESS..AND SOME OF IT IS NOT WHAT YOU THINK."

In order for the African-American adolescent and young adult males (or any adolescent or young adult male) to thrive in the community, it would interpersonal and community factors. Both internal and environmental factors are needed in order for the young adult to have a healthy progression to adulthood. Role models can foster the resiliency needed to assist with the process, and would serve as a direct contact with the adolescents and young adults. These specific role models would be exemplified as those worthy of being imitated and used as an example of a positive interpreter of well-being.

Community factors consist of school involvement, community activities, and church involvement. School involvement has focused mainly on academic standings.

TO THE LEADERS OF THE SCHOOLS: IF YOU DON'T TEACH A CHILD TO READ AT AN EARLY AGE, WHAT WILL YOU BE ABLE TO TEACH THEM AS AN ADOLESCENT OR YOUNG ADULT?

The success of adolescents and young adults in our communities have been directly correlated to their school environment, which minimizes and don't take seriously enough the emotional stress, drug use and violence which our adolescents and young adults face in the real world.

SHOW COMPASSION...SHOW AN INTEREST...SHOW THAT YOU CARE...

__T__EACH in the best way possible to help young people understand

__E__NCOURAGE a young person to their best potential.

__A__DMIRE them for the work that they do…and do well.

__C__ONNECT with each child…no matter how difficult the child.

__H__ELP each child…especially when you see that they need help.

This is what it's all about when we TEACH our children, adolescents and young adults. This is success. This is one way to keep our African-American adolescents and young adults stimulated and wanting them to come to school. Meet them where they are at and bring them the rest of the way. It can be done. It is possible. It has worked for so many of us. Because of that encouragement from teachers such as Mrs. Threet, Mr. Gardner, Mr. Seibles, Mr. Nelson, Mrs. Walker, Mrs. Jenkins, Mrs. Downings, many of us who became teachers and educators were able to give back and pay forward. It can't stop now. This is our calling. This is our ministry. These are our children, adolescents and young adults. ***For when love is not enough…we teach.***

Another community factor, which results in increased self-esteem and empowerment for our young adult male is church involvement. In my research, I have established a connection between church involvement and positive outcomes; self-esteem, psychological adjustment and relationship building have been directly correlated to church participation. I see this factor in my church every Sunday and throughout the week. I am blessed for my church and the way we do outreach for our young people. We have male role models present at all times and we give various options and activities that reaches out to the community at large. My church (Madison Avenue Christian

Reformed Church) has an outreach ministry center which meets the needs of the community. We have activities such as Cadets for the boys and adolescent young men. We have structured basketball teams for those young adults who need a place to hang out and be themselves without having to impress or meet society's expectations. They are greeted and mentored by the adult males of the church who are present and willing to step out on faith and work with our young adults. We have an outstanding after school program that meets the academic needs of the children and adolescents and encourages them to build from where they are at and move them forward. There are so many other programs that we offer, but when it comes to the adolescents and young adults, we have sessions where we meet with adolescents and young adults and share that special time with them to meet their needs and to invest the time needed in talking, praying and helping them through this journey in their lives. This is what the churches should be doing. This is a testimony to the belief that church is not just about "shoving God & Jesus down your throat " (as a couple of my young adults quote), but its about accepting them for who they are at this moment, listening to their stories, and meeting the need in a way that would encourage and give them hope.

The cognitive, formal framework of religion, not fitting into this type of setting, and not connecting with a church is a deterrent to almost every adolescent and young adult male. When an adolescent or young adult comes to my church, we have Pastor John who delivers the message that doesn't talk down to them, but includes them in on the topic for that Sunday. The sermons hit home for many them and they take what they have learned and try to practice it throughout the week. This is a big step. This is progress. This is the church becoming involved. *For when love is not enough...there is spiritual connectedness and outreach.*

CHAPTER TWELVE

"FROM ONE PARENT TO ANOTHER"

NOW A SPECIAL GIFT FOR MY PARENTS AND FOR THOSE WHO WILL AND HOPE TO BE PARENTS ONE DAY...

Parents...I want to make this a personal section for you, especially for those who are struggling with their adolescent and young adult males in your household. It is definitely a challenge raising young adult males. Most of the time, we perceive them as unappreciative, disrespectful, defiant and lazy. As a life coach for adults, families, adolescents and young adults, I deal with reality. When a person or family comes into my sessions, it is going to be about you....and only you....because everything begins with you. Once children come into your life...it is no longer about you. Let me say that sentence one more time...

ONCE CHILDREN COME INTO YOUR LIFE...IT IS NO LONGER ABOUT YOU...

Now in this session, it will be about you. So, act as though you are in one of my life coaching sessions and I ask you, "Why are you here?" "What is your purpose for "being present" here today?". The top number one answer is to establish a better rapport with my children...especially my teen age son/daughter. You tell me that you don't understand them and you would like to get help in getting through to them. Once you have given me that information I would have already known that it is not about them...it is all about you. You have the hardest job in the world...parenting. You now responsible for another person's life and that scares the hell out of you because of possible failures. We all have experienced this anxiety. Now instead of giving you the full seminar, I would like for you, the parent, to take the time and think about yourself. When I did my research, I asked these young adult males some specific questions that I would like for you to take the time and answer. You may find that the problems that are lacking in your children may be lacking in you...just to make sure that you got that statement...

"YOU MAY FIND THAT THE PROBLEMS THAT ARE LACKING IN YOUR CHILDREN MAY BE LACKING IN YOU..."

Get your pen or pencil ready and let's get started:

1. *How do you define Christian spirituality?*

    _____

    _____

    _____

2. *What does "coping" mean to you?*

   _____
   _____
   _____

3. *What method of coping do you use when it comes to anger?* _____

   _____
   _____
   _____

4. *What skills do you have to show spirituality as a way of coping?* _____

   _____
   _____
   _____

5. *How do you use spirituality in your everyday life?*

   _____
   _____
   _____

6. *At what point in time do you feel spirituality the most?*

   _____
   _____
   _____

7. *Give examples of when you have used spirituality as a way of coping.* _____

   _____
   _____
   _____

Now how did you do? Did you find many of these questions hard to answer? Did you find yourself not being able to answer these questions because none of them pertained to you? Or did you find yourself going through an "aha" moment? Many parents and families that I work with never took the time to think about their own spirituality, much less trying to teach their children about it. Many parents just assume that it begins in the church…Everything begins at home…

"MANY PARENTS ASSUME THAT SPIRITUALITY BEGINS IN THE CHURCH…EVERYTHING BEGINS AT HOME."

If you as a parent don't find peace and a center within yourself , the probably of your family falling apart is going to be very high. A lot of the blame game that families encounter is due to the fact that you do not have a release of your own…a place where you can go inside yourself and create that atmosphere of reconciliation and calm. Once you create that for yourself, your situations will have solutions and your family will come together. The biggest plus is that you will be able to become that role model that your child, adolescent and young adult can look up to and model after. That is your first step…creating the atmosphere for you and your family.

The next few steps are just reality checks, especially if you are a single parent and the other parent is no longer in the picture. Yes, this is a big problematic factor in the urban community. It is a reality that must be dealt with and I have some reality checkpoints that I would like to see you implement in your personal development and reunification of getting your young adult males back into the family and into the home structure. What I am about to say is probably going to get you mad, bring up old memories, and even have you put down this book…but keep reading…it gets better in helping you connect with your adolescent and young adult male.

1. ***Stop dragging your children into your past (Stop living your dream through your children)***

Somewhere along the way, as parents, we seemed to have dragged our children into our past. Let me clarify what I mean by this (even though most you who are reading this already know what I am talking about. Let's start with the most obvious factors. It was nice that as a child you wanted to be a dancer or a famous football player. Something happened where you never got that opportunity. You grow up and you and your partner have a child. So you say to yourself…"I want my child to be a dancer" or "I want my child to be a football player". So now you bring your child into your past and want them to now live your life through them.

DOES THIS SOUND FAMILIAR TO SOME OF YOU?

That is exactly what some of you are doing. If you really want to connect with your adolescent or young adult male, let them be what they want to become and support them in that vision. The reason why so many adolescent and young adult males may rebel is because of the fact that they are living in their parent's shoes and can't get out of them. There is definitely a difference between a parent's expectations of their children and living out your (parent's) dream through your children. We should expect our children to do what we tell them to do. It is also expected that they do well and achieve in school. This is the natural order of things. Having our children carry out our dreams and fantasies are not. This will cause great resentment and a divide in family unity. Children, adolescents and young adult males have their own dreams and goals. Let them fulfill them and support them in their success.

2. ***Stop treating your adolescent and young adult sons as your ex-relationships.*** In many life coaching sessions I had the families do an exercise where the mothers and sons(daughters) would imitate each other in an exercise that is entitled "Just like you". This exercise helped families see the way they see each other. In this particular session, I had the mothers imitate the sons and the sons imitate the mothers. This exercise revealed more than just imitating. This exercise revealed a lot of anger and a lot of hurt. It revealed a raw reality of what each mother and son was going through in the household. It also revealed a lot of clarity...especially for the mother. When the exercise began the main themes that kept coming out of the mouth of the sons while imitating the mothers were, "You are just like your no good father!!!", "You look and act just like that no good father of yours". At one point, you really couldn't tell the difference as to who were the parents because it became so real for them. The mothers in the room realized that they kept comparing their sons to their absent father. It wasn't until one of the young men that was in the circle came up to the son imitating the mother and grabbed him to "bring him down". The young man who saw the son imitating the mother was crying and it was hurting him more and more everytime he repeated those words. The more he said it, the more the tears came falling on his cheeks onto his clothes. It got so intense that the son of the mother he was imitating came out of character and cried out finally..."I can't get out of this f------ man's

shadow. The room fell silent while this young man cried out and sobbed beyond what one could imagine a young man crying in such pain while the other young man held him as if he was holding on for dear life, letting him know it was alright...he understood. The mother finally realized what she was doing to her son and this started the healing process for both of them. When she realized what was happening and what she was doing, she broke down and put her arms around both young men. That created a chain until everyone in the room became connected in that hug. Healing started taking place. Just to let you know, these families are now on the road to healing. The young man came back home and is now thriving. He is getting ready to graduate with his associate degree, but look what had to be done in order for healing to begin and the success became evident. The mother had to come to grips with the fact that her male son was his own entity...and not a clone of her ex-relationship. This leads to the next step to building that relationship with your adolescent and young adult son.

3.   ***Parents...LET GO OF THE PAST.*** This is one of the hardest things that adults have the hardest times doing. If you continue to hold on to all of this anger and hatred to those who have hurt you, you will never be able to be the best parent you can be. Parents carry around so much pain from their past that it becomes a part of the new family that you have made for yourself. Many times in life coaching sessions I hear, "I don't want to raise my kids like I was raised." How ironic that as they became parents, the same pattern was set. I decided in one of the sessions that I would take them

on some journeys. By the time the journeys were over, they had a new sense of purpose. They felt different about themselves and the life that they almost lost with their sons, because of the hatred they had for their male figures in their past relationships and growing up in the past with men in the family. The parents were transferring that hatred and anger to the sons. Instead of seeing their sons as a gift from God and raising them with love and encouragement, they were raising them with fear and contentment, believing that they would turn out like the other male counterparts in their long line of failed fathers and relationships. In order to learn about the journeys and take the journeys, you must become a part of my seminar...sorry. The two things that I can tell you in the book that can be a starting process for many families who wish to start that bonding process with their sons and build relationships again are: a) Read Psalm 139:14 and make this a declaration for yourself each morning you wake up and before you go to bed. It states:

Psalm 139:14 – "And I praise you because of the wonderful way you created me. Everything you do is marvelous! Of this I have no doubt."

Once you say this to yourself as a declaration and assurance to yourself, you will be able to see the best in your children...because you see the best in yourself. You are more than parents. You are specially made and by a God (Supreme Being) that saw something special in you to put you on this earth to give love and guidance to your next generation of those who will also be parents. You cannot undo the past that has been done to you, but you can correct the mistakes that are being made now, learn from them and build that bridge between your adolescent and young adult son.

The second thing is something you need to tell your adolescent and young adult sons. Tell them how special they are. If you cannot tell them by words, tell them by scripture. I have one you can tell them every day as your pledge in being an encouragement to them and letting them know how they matter to you and the purpose they serve in this world. That scripture will be Jeremiah 29:11, which states:

Jeremiah 29:11 – "I will bless you with a future filled with hope – a future of success, not of suffering." Now understand that you are building this bridge that has been broken for a little bit and your adolescent and young adult son may have a hard time at first when you tell them this. So, make it personal. Instead of saying "I", say "God". God has never failed him and if you really believe this as parents, God will see you through with the rest of His promise. This will lead me to the final step of connecting with your adolescent and young adult sons.

4. ***Develop a spiritual life together as a family.*** This step is the most difficult step because you will have to step out of your comfort zone from being non-existent in your son's life and begin a connection by taking simple steps to create a spiritual atmosphere. Throughout the day, make sure that you interact with your sons by asking him at least these following four questions: ***"How was your day?",*** If by chance he says "good", you follow up with, ***"I'm glad to hear that. What worked for you to make your day go so well?"*** This starts a conversation

going. It's positive and it gets better in time. If by chance he says something negative and if his day didn't go well, you would respond by saying, *"I'm sorry to hear that, son. What didn't work for you today?"*. By asking just these few questions, it opens up the door to building better relationships with your sons and shows your son that you are really focused on him and making sure that we commit to communicating on a daily basis. As your relationship builds, start saying to your son how thankful to God you are for having him as a son. Validate that he is loved and he is special.

ALL SONS...NO MATTER WHAT AGE WANTS TO HEAR THAT HE IS LOVED, VALUED AND SPECIAL.

To bring him into the next level...which is prayer, just say to him, *I have been praying for you and your safety, can I pray with you?* He may say "no" at first, but don't give up. Keep asking on a daily basis. Once you start praying and getting into the practice of talking to God every day, your son will see the difference in you and your behavior in how you treat him now and will start becoming more involved in the family and may begin praying with you. So, I will say this to you like God has told us many times..."I will not leave you nor forsake you". Use these words to remember not to give up on your adolescent or young adult males. Do not leave them nor forsake them. Be ever present. Be that parent that they need you to be...and I can assure you the best of results. *For when love is not enough... there is spirituality and unification in the family*

As a testimony as to what spirituality can do in the lives of the adolescent and young adult males in the urban community, I am presenting one of two actual studies I'd completed with 5 African-American young adult males. It is going to explain the purpose and the actual interview of all five young adult males in their journey through spirituality and coping. This is my research and my gift to you in the hope that you can embrace the world as seen by these young adult males and the many young adult males that they represent.

CHAPTER THIRTEEN

⤳

"FINAL THOUGHTS"

As I reflect on all that was written, I want everyone who reads this book to know that none of us are perfect parents or leaders. We make mistakes. Sometimes it is hard to admit when we are wrong as parents. Sometimes it is hard for other entities such as schools, churches, communities to admit, that we have failed our children, especially the adolescent and young adult males. I've learned something today from a dear friend through conversation and I would like to share this as a closing thought to help us remember about our adolescents and young adult males.

Our adolescent and young adult males need us. They won't let you know it. They won't give you the satisfaction of letting you know it…but then will blame you for not being there when they pushed you away so many times.

We have to remember that during these stages of their life, our young males are still being molded and need the love, encouragement, and a parent's unconditional love. But most of all, we need to show them spirituality…for when things go wrong and they need someone to go to when the world gives up on them, they decide to walk out and attempt to become their "own man" or even when they feel alone and abandoned with nowhere to go. They will need solace (comfort)…that special place to go, that they saw us go to when we were in despair. These adolescent and young adult males saw many of us go to that special place, whether it be in church or sitting in a chair at home with our heads bowed down. They may not have said anything, but I am sure that they've questioned it within themselves and wondered "why". Adolescents and young adult males don't necessarily have to receive this from home. As stated previous… some don't have that type of family environment. They could be the worst child in the world, and they do not need to live with you at home to show them that spirituality. It is our responsibility to love them, care for them and show them a better way through believing in someone bigger than ourselves. It starts with us. If our young men see that we believe that there is someone bigger than ourselves and start exercising faith first, this will change a young man's reason for living. This will change and transform adolescent and young adult males to a level of understanding that would make them want to be better. It would make them want to live better. It would help them even change the way they see us as parents and advocates.

Nothing happens overnight. Just don't give up on them. Stick with the process. As long as you instill spirituality within them, they may go astray…even stay away from you for a long period of time. But through all of the turmoil, trials and tribulations that these young men will go through while in "their valley" (deepest hurts), the overall outcome is that they will look up and know that there is someone bigger than themselves and will come back…and will always come back to what is right and true.

So when they do come back, don't tell them, "I told you so". Don't ask them, "What happened". Just be there when they come to the door...and welcome them in. When they come to the door, that is when you will know without a shadow of a doubt that *when love was not enough...spirituality worked.*

(Luke 15: 11-32)

APPENDIX

A Segment from "Spirituality and Coping of
the African-American Young Adult Male"
A Phenomenological Study

The purpose of this study was to examine the spirituality and coping of African American young adult males in the urban community. A small group of five African American young adult males were interviewed to examine how African American young adult males in the urban community connected and identified with a Christian base and also demonstrated how African American young adult males connected spirituality's support system in the community to strengthen coping skills. Using a small group of five African American young adult males granted the researcher the opportunity for eliciting intimate descriptions from each participant.

The phenomenological approach examines the in-depth experiences of the African American young adult male and the meanings that Christian experiences have for them. Phenomenological researchers, as qualitative researchers, are interested in meaning, but the phenomenological researcher additionally seeks to identify the essence of human experiences by understanding the lived experiences through the interpretation of the African American young adult male.

Consistent with this type of research, five African American young adult males from the urban community participated in this study. Participants were interviewed individually by the researcher. All interviews were audio taped. Throughout the interview process, the researcher assured the participants that all information used for this study would be strictly confidential and the participant's identity would be anonymous. All participants were able to receive a transcript of the audio taped interview to review for approval. Within the collection of this phenomenological research, the following information would generate comparisons of raw data from the interviews of the participants, along with common themes and observations worth noting throughout the interview process. In this study, the researcher served as the lead to data collection, analysis and interpretation.

Setting

This qualitative research study took place in the urban community of Paterson, New Jersey. The decision to conduct the research in Paterson was based on the fact that this researcher is a native Patersonian.

Participants

In this study, the sample of participants consisted of five African American young adult males residing in Paterson, New Jersey. Purposive sampling was the primary method of selecting participants who met the following criteria:

1. African American males.
2. Between the ages of 18-24.

3. A resident of the urban community.
4. Experienced in Christian spirituality within their growing process
5. Willing to participate in this particular research study.

Participants were selected through the posting of flyers throughout the public community bulletin boards in churches, community centers and community colleges throughout Paterson, New Jersey. A preliminary interview was scheduled for those participants who responded to the flyers posted. Each preliminary interviewed consisted of a presentation of the study that was to be conducted, which included an overview of the research study by the researcher and a copy of the informed consent, which was read by the researcher to the person being interviewed. This participant was given the informed consent for review, just in case the participant was selected for the study and had any additional questions. The participants selected were called back for a final interview, in which they had to bring back the informed consent form signed. Each participant received a copy of the signed informed consent. The formal interviews for the five participants selected were held in a multi-purpose room in the city of Paterson. Upon entering the multi-purpose room, each participant was served refreshments. Upon the completion of the interview, each participant waited to review the written transcript. Upon approval of the written transcript, the participant was given a $10.00 stipend, along with a "Thank you" card for their participation in this research study.

Research Questions

Using a qualitative phenomenological method for this study was the best approach in discovering the "what, how" and "why" of the questions that was asked and in understanding what the meanings of those shared experiences were to the African American young adult male.

The study posed the following research questions:

1. How do you define Christian spirituality?
2. What does coping mean to you?
3. What method of coping do you use when it comes to anger?
4. What skills do you have to show spirituality as a way of coping?
5. How do you use spirituality in your everyday life?
6. At what point in time do you feel spirituality the most?
7. Give example(s) of when you have used spirituality as a way of coping.

Data Collection and Analysis

The theory of this data analysis was based on the interviews of the participants. The interviews included verbal as well as non-verbal communication. Observations and field notes were also included into the interview process. Each participant was carefully observed as far as body language and facial expressions. The tone of the participant for each question was also monitored.

The participant timed each interview to be an hour. The first ten minutes consisted of the greeting from the researcher, a reminder about the purpose of the research, informed consent and the assurance of confidentiality between the researcher and the participant. Five minutes was allotted to the participant to tell the researcher a little bit about himself. This served as a stress releaser for the participant, and created a more comfortable situation for the actual interview. The first interview started on March 29, 2008 at 9:00 am, with the last interview concluding at 3:00

pm. The researcher engaged in conversation with the participant during refreshments until it was time for the formal interview to begin. Once the formal interview began, the researcher ceased all ideas, beliefs or assumptions relative to the participant's personal experiences.

As the formal interview commence, the researcher uses the process of *Epoche* to remove, or at least become aware of prejudices, viewpoints or assumptions regarding the phenomenon under investigation (Merriam, 1998) According to Merriam (1998), epoche requires that looking precede judgment and that judgment of what is "real" or "most real" be suspended until all the evidence (or at least sufficient evidence) is in. This break of judgment is crucial in phenomenological exploration and requires the setting aside of the researcher's point of view in order to see the experience for itself (Merriam).

The data analysis in this research study was based upon Moustakas' (1994) methodology of analyzing data through *Imaginative Variation,* having to do with trying to see the phenomenon from different lights or perspectives. Data analysis in this research was also based upon Creswell's (2003) methodology of analyzing data through observations, interviews and audio-visual materials. The researcher used transcriptions to establish themes found in data analysis. The researcher interviewed the participant, transcribed, listened, and analyzed the audio tapes. This process was done in this manner to protect the confidentiality of the participant, and maintain the agreement between the researcher and the participant. Each transcribed interview was read and analyzed to better comprehend the lived experience of the participant. Because of the privacy and protection of the five participants, each participant was assigned one of the following codes: Participant #1, Participant # 2, Participant # 3, Participant #4 and Participant # 5.

Presentation of Results

The data collected through the study participant's individual interview were analyzed using a concrete, step-by-step procedure (Hycner, 1985) in analyzing interview data. To include the method of phenomenological analysis of interview data, the collection, analysis, and presentation of data will be identical to the Hycner method of analysis of phenomenological data (Hycner, 1985) by practicing the following steps:

Step 1: Transcription

One of the most important steps in phenomenologically analyzing interview data is having the audio recording transcribed. This includes the accurate statements of each participant, noting vital non-verbal and para-linguistic communications (Hycner, 1985).

Step 2: Bracketing and the Phenomenological Reduction

The next step in the process involved listening to the audio recordings of each participant and reading the transcripts. This phenomenon meant developing an openness embracing whatever meanings appeared from the results of the audio recordings and transcripts. Through bracketing, the researcher suspended as much as possible, the researcher's meanings and interpretations and entered into the world of the participant who was interviewed. The researcher held the phenomenon for thorough inspection. It was taken apart and dissected. Its groundwork and basic structures were uncovered, defined and analyzed. This process meant understanding the meaning of what the participant was saying, rather than what the researcher expected the person to say (Hycner, 1985).

Once the researcher bracketed the past experiences and knowledge, the researcher interviewed the five African American male participants. The interviews were conducted by using a list of questions that was created in advance by the researcher. The questions were created to provide structure to the interview process that was equable for each participant.

Step 3: Listening to the Interview for a Sense of the Whole

After completion of the interviews, the researcher transcribed all five tape-recorded interviews word for word or verbatim. These transcriptions became the data for the study. To analyze this data the researcher involved one's self in listening to the entire tape several times as well as reading the transcripts a number of times. This provided a context for the visibility of specific units of meaning and themes. While doing this, the researcher especially want to listen to the non-verbal and para-linguistic levels of communication, that is, the intonations, the emphases, the pauses, etc. (Hycner, 1985).

Step 4: Delineating Units of General Meaning

During this phase the researcher is required to make an ample amount of judgment calls while consciously bracketing his own presuppositions in order to avoid bias or misinterpretation (Creswell, 2003). At this point, the researcher begins the task of going over every word, phrase, sentence, paragraph and noted significant non-verbal communication in the transcript in order to evoke the participant's meanings (Hycner, 1985). The researcher found that most of the interviews exhibited numerous body gestures, postures and verbal dialect, which will be described later in the chapter.

Step 5: Delineating Units of Meaning Relevant to the Research Question

In this process, the researcher is ready to address the research question to each participant. The researcher addresses the research question to this unit of general meaning to ascertain whether what the participant has said acknowledges and clarifies the research question.

Step 6: Eliminating redundancies

The process of eliminating redundancies look over the list of units of relevant meaning and discard those, which are clearly repetitive to others previously listed. It is important to understand the actual number of times a unit of relevant meaning was stated since that in itself might indicate some importance (Hycner, 1985). Non-verbal and para-linguistic warning signals, which seem to emphasize or alter meaning of the words should also be taken into account. This could very well change the context (Hycner).

Step 7: Cluster Units of Relevant Meaning

Through this process, the researcher attempts to determine whether there seems to be some common theme or essence that strengthens discrete units of relevant meaning. At this stage, the essence appeared to have more to do with the "knowing" or realization that occurred (Hycner, 1985).

Step 8: Determining Themes from Clusters of Meaning

This is the final process where the researcher cross-examines all the clusters of meaning to discover if there is one or more central themes which expresses the essence of these clusters (Hycner, 1985). This identification allows the researcher to examine for common themes, different perspectives and different levels of experience of the participants.

Step 9: Writing A Summary for Each Individual Interview

Once the above steps have been completed, the researcher reviews the interview transcript and writes up a summary of the interview. This would incorporate the themes that have been evoked from the data (Hycner, 1985).

Step 10: Return to the Participant with the Summary and Themes

It is important for the researcher to conduct a "validity check", by inviting the participant to return to engage in dialogue with the participant concerning what the researcher has found at this point. This was done one day after the original interview took place. The written summary and themes were provided to the participant. (Hycner, 1985).

Step 11: Modifying Themes and Summary

This section would only be utilized if the researcher finds reason to change any information following a return and dialogue with the participant.

Step 12: Identifying General and Unique Themes For All the Interviews

The researcher at this point would note if there are any themes common with most of the interviews. If there are, then these themes from the individual interviews can be clustered together, indicating a general theme that resulted from most or all of the interviews (Hycner, 1985). The researcher would also note when there are themes that are outstanding to a single interview or a minority of the interviews (Hycner).

Step 13: Contextualization of Themes

After the general and unique themes have been observed, it is helpful to place these themes back within the overall contexts from which these themes emerged (Hycner, 1985). This allows the researcher to let the participant convey their experience through their own course aside from any intention or control on their part.

Step 14: Composite Summary

Finally, a composite summary of all the interviews is written. By doing this one would accurately capture the essence of the phenomenon being investigated (Hycner, 1985).

Descriptive Narratives of the Lived Experiences

Participant # 1

Participant # 1 is a 22 year-old African American male, who is a product of a single grandparent environment, being raised by his grandmother since the age of five, after the death of his mother. He has no recognition or father figure in his life. The only thing he knew about his mother was that she was in prison when he was a baby, and she died when he was in kindergarten, right after being released from prison. His life centered around his grandmother and church. Participant # 1's body language spoke of confidence of having a grandmother who kept him in church and taught him about being a Christian. His body posture shifted erect as he spoke about his grandmother. His facial expression shifted from serious to a hint of a smile, which suggested a happy moment in his life. The tone of his voice commanded attention from the researcher, speaking direct and with authority as he spoke about his grandmother's teachings. His eyes would show a peace of mind that helped him to realize that being spiritual is what makes him successful in his life. His interview was conducted in the following manner:

Participant # 1

Researcher: How do you define Christian spirituality?

Participant # 1: I define spiritual. . .or Christian spirituality as the concept of love and to do unto others as you would like them to do unto you. I define Christian spirituality as serving humanity and the social and economical community. I think of the concept of the trinity: Father, Son and the Holy Spirit. I think of integrity, righteousness and justice. Christian spirituality is humbling yourself in order to do God's will for His kingdom. Christianity is not existentialism. Christian spirituality believes that God has a plan for my life and always thinking of others gives me a sense of Christian spirituality.

Researcher: What does coping mean to you?

Participant # 1: Coping to me, is the psychologically clearing of one's mind of the issues and problems and dealing with them at the same time. Coping is a very spiritual. . .a very spiritual thing and helps clean one's problems from the psyche.

Researcher: What method of coping do you use when it comes to anger?

Participant # 1: I use the method of patience and the exploring of all the perspectives before I act with my emotions. I try to be as ad...objective as possible, and not to attack individual people when faced with uncomfortability or anger.

Researcher: What skills do you have to show spirituality as a way of coping?

Participant # 1: The skills that I possess in spirituality as a way of coping is praying to God, having patience and having the universal concept of unconditional love. Praying to God helps me cope with the everyday issues, vicissitudes of life and thinking of others while reflecting upon my day. I portray patience as a way of coping and the universal concept of love where I love people in spite of the wrongs or the inconsistencies of one's self. I love them in spite of everything or anything that they have done that violates spiritual teachings.

Researcher: How do you use spirituality in your everyday life?

Participant # 1: The way that I use spirituality in an everyday life is by seeking self-knowledge of myself that incorporates the mind, body and soul, understanding how everything in life is connected from God's creation, in nature and to the subreme. . .the supreme spirit of God.

Researcher: At what point in time do you feel spirituality the most?

Participant # 1: The point where I feel spirituality the most is when I look at nature and the complexity of the human body. Creation of the world itself helps me as a spiritual temple where

Grr...where God dwells within me feel connected to nature that God has created and the connection between the organic nature of my body, in unison with that.

Researcher: Give example (s) of when you have used spirituality as a way of coping.

Participant # 1: Some of the examples that I use in spirituality in coping would be one, in performing poetry, in the sense that spirituality helps me cope while expressing my thoughts and my emotions through writing, which is a form of my internal self. Secondly, physical or the physical. . .the physically exercising aspect is another way I show spirituality coping because I release a lot of frustration and vexation in dealing with the problems. Another example would be expressing my feelings to God by praying and expressing those feelings to family and friends, especially the spiritual leaders that I follow by watching their spiritual sermons and pondering upon what was said spiritually.

Participant # 2

Participant # 2 is a 21 year-old African American male. He is a product of a two-parent household. Participant # 2 displayed a sense of confidence in his erect posture. Erect posture is generally associated with higher spirits, greater confidence, and more openness (McKay, Davis & Fanning, 1983). He contributes that to parental and spiritual guidance. Both parents were involved in the community and attended church with the family regularly. Being that Participant # 2s' parents stressed positive feedback, it was evident in his interview. . .even at the points when there was evidence of stress and a slight sense of uneasiness. Through Participant # 2's body language, there were times when just thinking positive wasn't enough. Points throughout the interview showed him at a loss for words and reaching for the positive words that was embedded within himself through his parent's influence and not his spiritual senses.

During the refreshment period, Participant # 2 spoke of some of the knowledge he received from his parents, which were similar to the words used when he was at a loss for words in his formal interview. His interview was conducted in the following manner:

Researcher: Question # 1: How do you define spirituality?

Participant # 2: Well first and foremost it's, uh, having faith in our Lord and Savior. Umm, it's living a clean, repentful life and you know it's also about making impact on other peoples' lives, and not just your own. Umm, a lot of people in today's community, they, um, you know, they figure that if they live a clean life, uh, you know, and go to church on a daily basis then they'll get a piece of the pie in Heaven. However, I, I beg to differ because it's not just affecting yourself but it's uh, you know, affecting the people around you.

Researcher: Question # 2: What does "coping" mean to you?

Participant # 2: Well "coping" means to me that …you have to find a way to deal with the problems by any means necessary. Umm…It means going around different obstacles…uh. . .going through many barriers in life…umm. . .and I feel that coping is dealt with by surrounding yourself with a group of positive people as well as role models to look up to. And, I feel that coping is an essential factor in life that everybody has to go through in order to succeed.

Researcher: Question # 3: What method of coping do you use when it comes to anger?

Participant # 2: The first method that I naturally use is to. . .you know…stay by myself, think things over and I leave it inside my chest. Umm…this is the natural way I do things, but it is not the most productive. Uhh…the most productive I would say is to let your anger vent by talking to people that you can trust and people that offer good advice.

Researcher: Question # 4: What skills do you have to show spirituality as a way of coping?

Participant # 2: Well...umm...umm...you know...despite how bad of a...a day you could have had...umm...you know...having faith and a spirituality, I think that...uhh...prevail over you and help you make it to the next day. Umm...every night I personally pray before I go to sleep. Umm...I pray for all the good things in my life and I also pray upon all the things that I need to...you know... improve. And, I think spirituality ...you know...it helps you, it motivates you, and it pushes you to achieve ...uhh...more goals and ...uhh... push you to the next plateau.

Researcher: Question # 5: How do you use spirituality in your everyday life?

Participant # 2: I use spirituality in my everyday life by waking up in the morning and just telling myself I want to live my life today with the...you know...having the most impact on the society around me. Umm...its not just...you know...something that I do personally, but...umm...you know...I think it's the...the best to...to improve the community around you and society around you as well.

Researcher: Question # 6: At what point in time do you feel spirituality the most?

Participant # 2: I feel spirituality the most when ...when I'm down. Umm...I feel it the most because I feel like I don't have anybody else to rely on...you know...there's not always people around. So...you know...with spirituality, something that's always going to be there for you. Umm...you know...I do feel it in my ... my good times, too, but sometimes you need that extra drive and that push to push you to the next level.

Researcher: Question # 7: Give example(s) of when you have used spirituality as a way of coping.

Participant # 2: Uhh...one example would be...umm...I'd say about six weeks ago. I pulled my hamstring running track and... you know...I thought it was going to be the end of my season and I was really upset and I was very depressed. Umm...you know...I had faith...uhh...I kept talking to people. People were talking me through it and...you know...I was praying every night, and I always look for the...the positives of...you know...having a injury. And... uhh...you know... spirituality was something that's always there... you know...it's...it's an important factor in my life and that took a lot of weight and depression of my shoulders.

Another example was in...in high school. I actually...you know...got up...caught up in a...a really dramatic situation where I thought I had a girl pregnant and spirituality...you know...would help me get through that, as well. I couldn't really talk to my parents about it...my friends...you know...it was a battle I was fighting on my own. And, the only other thing I had on my side was...was spirituality. I used to find myself in church parking lots at 2:00 am in the morning, praying and...you know...just talking to myself... trying to talk myself through things.

Participant # 3

Participant # 3 is a 20 year-old African American male. This participant displayed anxiety. During the refreshment period, Participant # 3 conveyed a feeling of apprehension, uneasiness, concern and worry that was accompanied by heightened physical arousal. Through his anxiety, Participant # 3 still wanted to tell his story of how he grew up spirituality and how being faithful in his walk with Christ, helped him to overcome adversity. The look on his face and his body expression showed a very tense, but determined young man, who described his lived experience as a negative chain of events. His parents were very strict in the religion of Islam. Participant # 3 decided that when he became old enough to decide his faith, he would choose Christianity. Because of this discrepancy between him and his parents, this caused such a family divide that Participant # 3 left the family and depended on his faith in God. Through the support of his church and other family members, he survived by entering college, and became dedicated in his poetry writing as a way of coping. His interview was conducted in the following manner:

Researcher: How do you define Christian spirituality?

Participant # 3: I define Christian spirituality as a pursuit of the teachings of Jesus Christ. It can go from following from the Holy Bible itself or from its interpreters such as priests and the pope and other people in higher places.

Researcher: What does coping mean to you?

Participant # 3: Coping is to deal with issues or problems in a way of resolving them. It can go from either talking about it or taking it out and dealing with it. In certain cases, you might have to agree to disagree. The end result of coping would be having found a way to resolve your problem.

Researcher: What method of coping do you use when it comes to anger?

Participant # 3: At the younger age, I would cope with my anger through physical means because I was immature and I felt expressing it by hitting something or taking it out and punishing something would resolve it. The positive side of that would be taking it to the gym instead of getting into a fight. As I progressed, I learned to communicate. By this means, I would express how I feel with my friends and family and in return make bonds with them. Eventually, I got into spoken word and poetry, which let me express exactly how I feel whenever way I do and at the same time, other people heard me, so it felt like I made a difference. Sometimes the crisis would be so big where I can't write about it, work out or even talk it out and I would just have to cry it out.

Researcher: What skills do you have to show spirituality as a way of coping?

Participant # 3: Communication would be my best answer to the way of coping in a spiritual sense. Whether I commute...

communicate with God or people around me, I always…umm…get something out and resolve something and at the same time, learn and its just a good way of sharing.

Researcher: How do you use spirituality in your everyday life?

Participant # 3: I definitely use spirituality in my everyday life at times when things are down because when you have nobody else to look to, you always have God and at other times when I am extremely excited or happy, I always have to find a way to thank God. I also find at times that when I'm spiritual for no reason, that's my strongliest connection with God, cause I don't have a reason or excuse to talk to Him. But, I still do, and that showses my appreciation to God.

Researcher: At what point in time do you feel spirituality the most?

Participant # 3: On a daily basis, I feel spirituality the most when I wake up and go to sleep because that is the beginning and end of the day, and God is the first and last thing that comes to mind. On.. in a broader sense, spirituality effects me the most when I'm being distracted and still look at God.

Researcher: Give example(s) of when you have used spirituality as a way of coping.

Participant # 3: I use spirituality as a way of coping when things are out of my hand. For example, if I take a test that I studied for, and I know I'm going to get a certain grade, but I'm not really sure, I start praying to God cause it's not really in my hands. Another time I would use spirituality to cope would be when I'm feeling sick or a family member's feeling sick cause I have no way of helping them or knowing how they're going to get better.

The best example of using spirituality to cope was…umm… when I didn't have a place to stay because I had to leave home and I had friends and family…I had enough friends and family to turn to and talk to, but it was a spiritual sense that I had to connect with

God because I had to break a connection with my parents (which was the hardest) and I knew I eventually would have to make that bond again. But, it was a making of the bond that would be the hardest part.

At times like this when I feel like I don't have family, I still have God who seems to be the answer for everything.

Participant # 4

Participant # 4 is a 19 year-old African American male who is a product of a two family household. The household consists of the biological mother and a stepfather. Participant # 4 was what one would consider a "hard-core street thug" with a lot of street life experience. The participant shared that he had been in and out of shelters as a retaliation of his biological father leaving his mother and the family structure change when his stepfather came into the picture. Participant # 4 raised his little sister as his mother went to work. He was considered as the "man of the house" when his father left. When his stepfather came into the picture, he saw himself as no longer a helper, but a hinderance. Even though he kept getting in trouble with the law, the one thing that Participant # 4 remembered was going to church as a child with his grandmother and always remembering the words "God will take care you. Just put your trust in Him". He still struggles with the family structure, but sees spirituality as his way of coping. His interview was conducted in the following manner:

Researcher: How do you define Christian spirituality?

Participant # 4: Well to me...umm...Christian spirituality, as far as being a Christian, it's more of...of a job. You come in, do your work, you know what you have to do, you know the laws that you have to live by as far as being a Christian. As far as spirituality comes into play, now they both go hand in hand because you can't ha...you can't be a Christian and not have a spirituality to go with it. Now as far as

...as far as walking with God and knowing which path you have to take, that pretty much says you're a Christian, but not everybody is a Christian being that you just hold a title. You have to live by it day by day. We all slip up. We all fall, but being able to know that you can depend on God in any way, which way or form...umm...basically states...you know...the...umm...Christian spirituality.

Researcher: What does coping mean to you?

Participant # 4: Well, coping mean to me, it basically has... you know...two different types of forms. Coping is, as far as what you can do to help yourself get through something, or it can be the advice you get from someone else to help you get through anything that you're going through. As far as with yourself, it could be more of a spiritual type of way you can go through it. It can be more of a... umm...a mental state that you can go through it...umm...you can also talk to yourself, which most people seems...you know...since you don't have nobody to talk to, sometimes that's the best way, or either you can write it down.

Another way as far as...you know...getting advice from people, you can take in whatever you want to hear from anybody...you know...most people have different ways of doing it, which...you know...is better for you. So, you can, kind of like...you know... shuffle through them and find out which way fits you the best.

Researcher: What method of coping do you use when it comes to anger?

Participant # 4: As far as coping when I'm angry...umm...I usually just...you know...umm...end up doing something like as far as either going to the gym, which I like to do or...you know...go out and play football or hang out with my friends...you know...as far as to get...ease my mind because anger can also build up, which can cause...you know...umm...destruction within yourself if you don't let it out in some type of way or form...you know...without harming somebody...right... and such as that.

Researcher: What skills do you have to show spirituality as a way of coping?

Participant # 4: For the skills that I have is basically I'm a good listener. Another one is I'm always...you know...interacting with people...you know...I'm more...I'm outspoken, meaning that as when you're outspoken...umm...people like to talk to somebody like that, meaning that...you know...you're not all to yourself. You can talk back to them if they talk to you. Another thing is...umm... I'm very...umm...kind-hearted. People love to come around me... umm...open-hearted.

Researcher: How do you use spirituality in your everyday life?

Participant # 4: As far as using spirituality in my everyday life... umm...at one point you have to understand as you get closer to God that everything...you gotta take the good and the bad, meaning with the good you still have to exalt Him and praise Him. With the bad, you can't just be mad...say, "Oh, it's the devil!" And, it's not always him, always...you know...so you gotta give God a praise through the good and the bad. So, as far as...you know...me using that in my everyday life, just like the normal people...you know...you wake up, ask God, "Thank you for waking me up this morning."...you know...umm...give you safe traveling mercies on your way going to work and such as that. Umm...as far as with me, I...I won't say... you know...that...umm...as far as...you know...using it every hour on the hour, but I do exalt Him every chance I get.

Researcher: At what point in time do you feel spirituality the most?

Participant # 4: The time when I feel spirituality the most is when I am going through something, before I go through something and when I come out of it because the most...the most you see people going through something, they're going to start praying as they're going through their...going through the trials and tribulations, and they can't be like that, cause that's what...it's normal. That's what...

you know…already's been said, already been shown…you know… that's what most people go through. So, as far as with me, it's before I go through it and once I come out of it, cause that's when all the glory, and you can raise your hands and reign in victory.

Researcher: Give example(s) of when you have used spirituality as a way of coping.

Participant # 4: As times when I use coping as a way of spirituality, as far as…you know…umm…when I feel like I can't go through something on my own…you know…I drop down and try to get some answers from God in prayer. But…umm…as it's been said…you know… the same power that's invested in Him, He also gave to us, meaning…you know…God won't always be right there. Sometimes He'll put you out on a limb just to see if you can do it on your own, and…umm…that's the most time when I use coping as far as with spirituality… when I'm praying. Another time I use it…umm…when I'm uplifted in everything…you know…just to give…go inside the church and just to feel the brotherly and sisterly love. That's another thing as far as coping, which will bring you back down to earth, especially when you're going through something. Just a simple hug, alone, can also bring you through anything that you're going through at the time.

Participant # 5

Participant # 5 is an 18 year-old African American male. Participant # 5 is a product of a single foster mother, who eventually adopted him as a young child. Being abused as a child, he became a very anxious and nervous child. Throughout the interview you will note the many times where he has stuttered to get his point across. This form of language would happen when Participant # 5 get excited about telling his lived experiences. Growing up with his single adoptive mom, he has always found the blessings in life. His body gesture and the continuous smile that was on his face through the whole interview process told the story of a young man who embraces life. He goes to church services on most Sundays, and has been doing it for as long as he could remember. God is the focus of his life and he lives the life of spirituality through his walk with Christ. Here is how Participant # 5 conducted his interview:

Researcher: How do you define Christian spirituality?

Participant # 5: I define Christian spirituality as…uhh…this… if…for…it's…it's how you walk. It's…it's your walk in Christ and… and how you deal with it. Like, everybody has a…a different walk and they talk to God different ways, but it's…it's your…your level of spirituality that you have with God and it's just…it's dealt in all different ways and different Christians, and I…I…I just see it as your walk with God and being true to it. That's the main thing is to be true to it. And, that's what I see that as.

Researcher: What does coping mean to you?

Participant # 5: Coping means to me…it's uhh…again…how each Christian deals with their struggles, some problems. It's like, you can say problems, but…you know…as a real Christian they been through a lot and somewhat of a struggle because anybody can just, like go through a problem and get through it easy, but a struggle is a little harder and like, church and Christian terms and it's…it's…it's like, you use God to get through your struggles and if you cope that way, then…you know…you…you…you always come out on top. So, that's what coping is to me, like, using, like…ahh…not using God, but…you know…asking God for help and just getting through your problems with the Christian way.

Researcher: What method of coping do you use when it comes to anger?

Participant # 5: The method of coping I use when it comes to anger is isolation, as in just me and God. It's…I…I…I think more Christians should do that, just isolate yourself with just you and God. And, that's my method because it…it calms you down and you can see clearly and…you know…you don't see through the…the anger lens and…you know…just whatever your…your situation is when you're angry just…just isolate yourself with just you and God. That's my method of coping.

Researcher: What skills do you have to show spirituality as a way of coping?

Participant # 5: Umm…I use it in a way…like…it's…it's different variations of it. Like…like communication is one. Like…like…you know…God gave me…like…the gift of…like…communication… like…I can communicate… like…good and it's like you got…you have to know how to communicate people with people when they're mad or like when they're going through struggles or like any… any type of situation. And…uhh…like being kind-hearted…you know…cause God…God is kind, patient, loving. So…like…you know…when you look in the mirror, its…you…you are God…or you're a reflection of God. So…you know…you just do as he would do and…you know… that's what I would try to do.

Researcher: How do you use spirituality in your everyday life?

Participant # 5: One of the ways I use spirit…spirit…spirituality in my everyday life is praying. You know…praying everyday…maybe not everyday, but praying a lot to God and…and uhh…just talking to him and reading…reading the word. And I…I talk to much of my peers. I…I…I …I do that more than anything…talk amongst your peers about God…about your …you know…your spirituality life and…and church and that's what I use.

Researcher: At what point in time do you feel spirituality the most?

Participant # 5: I feel it the most in my struggles. It's because that's when I…I…I tend…that's when I…for me…that's when I…I…I tend to want Him more…like connect with Him more. Uhh…it's just like…you know…as in needing him more. Like… you…like He's with you in your…your joys and your sorrows, but when you struggle, you tend to call on God just a little harder than you normally would. So…you know…that's when I just…you know…feel that.

Researcher: Give example(s) of when you have used spirituality as a way of coping.

Participant # 5: Umm…I've used it as coping…like….uhh…I'm going to stick to the anger…like when…like I'm angry or mad, I would…umm…go to the church and just throw on some acoustic headphones and grab a pair of sticks and just like…just play unto God…like…or just play out anger without unto God…or….and I would just…like just play my heart out, even get on the piano and just play…like…gospel songs…like…songs that…like…I was feeling then, that would help me out…just play them on the piano and then… you know…just talk to God after it…and that's how I cope out.

Qualitative Data Analysis: Some Common Themes

How do you define spirituality?	1	2	3	4	5
The concept of love	X				
To do unto other(as you would like them to do unto you)	X				
Serving humanity and the social and economical community (making an impact on other peoples' lives)	X	X			
The concept(teachings) of the Trinity: (Father, Son, and the Holy Spirit)	X		X	X	
Integrity, righteousness and justice	X				X
Humbling yourself in order to do God's will for His Kingdom	X				
Not existentialism	X				
Walking with God (following the plan (path) He has for your life)	X			X	X
Always thinking of others	X	X			
Having Faith in our Lord and Savior	X	X		X	X
Living a clean, repentful life (daily)		X		X	
A job				X	
Being a Christian				X	

Table # 1: Breakdown of Question 1: How do you define spirituality?

The group data for question # 1 of the formal interview, *"How do you define spirituality?"* explored several findings. Four out of the five participants defined spirituality as *"Having faith in our Lord and Savior"*. Participant # 1 uses the phrases, "the concept of the trinity: Father, Son and the Holy Spirit" and stating that "God has a plan for my life…" to affirm his faith in spirituality. Participant # 2 actually stated the phrase "having faith in our Lord and Savior". Participant # 4 uses the phrase, "being able to know that you can depend on God in any way, which way or form" as his confirmation of having faith. One observation that the researcher realized that may have caused a little concern was that of Participant # 3. Before the formal interview began, we had a chance to talk during the refreshment period, and he gave a testimony of his faith in Jesus Christ and how Jesus Christ has brought him this far in his life. But as we began the interview, the researcher noticed a disturbing look on his face, which may have been one of betrayal or dishonor to his family. He talked of his family's struggle with his newly found spirituality that he practices and he may still feel an obligation to his parents and their spirituality. His body gesture exhibited some anxiety, which didn't change his interview, but changed the power of his formal interview.

Three out of the five participants stated "Walking with God" and "The concept (teachings) of the Trinity" as a way of also defining spirituality. Walking with God was an important statement for Participants 1, 4, and 5. Participant # 1 spoke with the researcher during the refreshment period and used the term "humbling" as a way of walking with God. He felt that in order to walk with God, he had to walk in the spirit of "humbleness". He used this in his formal interview. Participant # 4 stated that, "You have to live it day by day" (referring to walking with God and knowing which path you have to take). Participant # 5 demonstrated a body gesture of confidence that confirmed his statement "…it's how you walk. It's your walk in

Christ and…and how you deal with it…your walk with God and being true to it." Participant # 5 also used a lot of hand gestures that suggested an excitement of being able to live his story through his interview. The smile on his face portrayed a look of happiness that was beyond that this researcher could put into words.

The concepts (teachings) which defined spirituality for Participants 1, 3, and 4 were in terms of integrity, righteousness and justice (for Participant # 1), following from The Holy Bible or from its interpreters (for Participant # 3), and Participant # 4 used the example of a job: "You come in, do your work, you know what you have to do, you know the laws that you have to live by as far as being a Christian." Participant # 4 presented a body gesture of "arrogance", as almost defending his lifestyle, for being raised in the streets, and having to defend his manhood. He wanted to make sure that this researcher did not see him as just a "street thug", but someone who loved God and believed in his spirituality "his way".

What does coping mean to you?	1	2	3	4	5
Psychological clearing of one's mind	X				
A very spiritual thing (Asking God to get through your struggles)	X				
Having to find a way to deal with problems (resolving issues by any means necessary	X	X	X	X	X
Surrounding yourself with positive people (i.e., role models)		X			
An essential factor in life that everybody has to go through in order to succeed		X			
Receiving advice from someone else to help you get through anything you're going through				X	

Table # 2: Breakdown of Question 2: What does coping mean to you?

What method of coping do you use when it comes to anger?	1	2	3	4	5
Patience	X				
Exploring all perspectives before acting on emotions	X	X	X	X	X
Isolating one's self (staying by yourself)		X			
Leave it inside my chest		X			
Talking to people that you can trust (offers good advice)		X			
Through physical means			X	X	
Communication			X		

Table # 3: Breakdown of Question 3: What method of coping do you use when it comes to anger.

In this particular breakdown, the researcher found that each participant explored some type of coping perspective before acting on emotion. In the case of participant # 1, patience was his main focus of coping when it came to anger. It was participant # 1 who coined the phrase *"exploring all perspectives before acting on emotions."* This phrase helped this researcher to find the common thread that linked these participants together for this particular question. For participant # 2, staying to himself thinking things over was a method for coping when it came to anger. Participant # 2 showed the willingness to talk to people that he trusted and offered good advice as another method of coping when it came to anger. This expression was demonstrated through his body gesture. This participant expressed a sense of warmth in his body gesture and displayed a confidence in his posture as he talked about the people in his life that helped him through his spiritual journey during our refreshment part of the interview.

Participant # 3 used communication through spoken word and poetry. This young adult male would express his method of coping by communicating through writing, working, talking or crying it out when the crisis became too overwhelming. Participant # 4 would go the gym, play football or hang with his friends as a coping mechanism for anger. This young adult male always believed that this is what saved him many times from going to jail. Physical activity prevented him from doing harm to someone else and created another way to vent his anger.

Participant # 5 expressed using God to get through the struggles of coping with anger. He refers to it as "isolation with just him and God". By isolating himself, it helped him to think and see clearly, creating an environment of calm, knowing that God was in control of the situation.

What skills do you have to spirituality as a way of coping?	1	2	3	4	5
Prayer life	X				
Patience	X				X
Unconditional love	X				X
Faith		X			
Spirituality		X			
Communication			X	X	X
Outspoken				X	
Kind/Open Hearted				X	X

Table # 4: Breakdown of Question 4: What skills do you have to show spirituality as a way of coping?

The one key factor with *Table # 4* was the fact that communication was the only skill that showed the most consistent pattern with these participants. For participants 3, 4, and 5, communicating with God (or the people around them) was a key skill they possessed as a way of coping. Participant # 4 considered himself to be a "good listener", which constitutes as a major contributor in communication skills. Listening is an essential skill for making and keeping relationships. Listening is a commitment (McKay, Davis & Fanning, 1983). It is a commitment to understanding how people feel and see their world. It means putting aside your own prejudices and beliefs, anxieties and self-interest, so that one can step behind the other person's eyes (McKay, Davis & Fanning). Participant # 5 interprets this skill as a gift from God, and sees himself as a reflection of God through communication. Participant # 5 also uses the fruits of the spirit from the Holy Bible as a reflection of whom he is when communicating: kind, patient and loving. This researcher has come to recognize that if Participant # 5 communicates through the fruits of the spirit, then Participant # 1 should be included into the skill of communication. In order to communicate, one must also possess patience, which is also one of the fruits of the spirit. Participant # 1 portrayed patience, as a way of coping, where he can communicate with people in spite of the wrongs or the inconsistencies of one's self...unconditionally. The red "X", symbolizing Participant # 1 in parentheses was placed as resource to leave the reader to acknowledge and come to their own conclusion.

How do you use spirituality in your everyday life?	1	2	3	4	5
When seeking self-knowledge (awareness)	X	X			
When understanding how everything in life is connected to God	X			X	
When making an impact on the society/community around me		X			X
When showing appreciation to God			X	X	
When times are down (needing God the most)			X		
Praying					X
Reading the Bible (The Word)					X
Communicating God to others (peers, etc.)					X

Table # 5: Breakdown of Question 5: How do you use spirituality in your everyday life?

There were no major findings in *Table # 5* that would connect a major amount of interview participants with one answer. However, two things started to emerge through observation of the participants. One, when asking this question, the researcher really noted the different genre of young adult African American males that he selected for this research project. As this researcher observed how each participant answered this question, this researcher noticed one major similarity. While answering this question, every participant shifted their posture from an upright posture to a slumped posture, as if they were in deep thought and really needed to think about this particular question. Usually exhibiting a slumped posture suggests a sign of feeling "low", fatigued, or inferiority" (McKay, Davis & Fanning, 1983. This was not the case with any of the five participants. Participants 2, 4, & 5 slumped into the chair, looking up into space as if they were searching for God's approval. When a person looks upward they are often thinking. In particular they are probably making pictures in their head and thus may well be an indicator of a visual thinker. Participants # 1 slumped down with his head facing down, as if he was praying for an answer. Looking down can be a signal of submission. It can also indicate that the person is feeling guilty. Participant # 3 just gave a gazed stare with his hands holding his face, looking downward towards the floor, contemplating. The moment before they began to answer this particular question was when this researcher gained his second realization. Each of the participants spoke with hope in their heart. All of the participants, once again, shifted their body posture to the upward position and began to reveal their answer in a way that changed the way this researcher saw them as African American young adult males.

At what point do you feel spirituality the most?	1	2	3	4	5
When seeking self-knowledge (awareness)	X				
Looking at God through nature	X				
Looking at God through the complexity of the human body	(X)				
When facing trials and tribulations	(X)	X	X	X	X
When I am alone	(X)	X	X	X	X
When celebrating	(X)	X	X	X	X

Table # 6: Breakdown of Question 6: At what point do you feel spirituality the most?

The breakdown of *Table # 6* examined all five participants experiencing spirituality the most when they were faced with trials and tribulations. Participant # 1 spoke before the formal interview and commented on this very topic. Participant # 1 did not use the same word phrasing for his formal interview, as he talked about his spirituality during the refreshment period. When talking about his spirituality while having refreshments, he made the comment that he embraces spirituality all of the time and needed it especially when he was going through problems in his life. When the actual interview question, *"At what point do you feel spirituality the most?"* was asked to Participant # 1, he responded by saying that he feels spirituality the most when "he looks at nature and the complexity of the body" which may be interpreted as the trials and tribulations a body experiences. This can be expressed through being alone and celebrating. However, the researcher put an "X" in parentheses to give account of what Participant # 1 interpreted during the formal interview, correlating with the top two answers given in the above table.

One point that was made evident in *Table # 6*, was that all five of the participants interviewed experienced spirituality the most when facing trials and tribulations, when they are alone, and when celebrating life. Participant # 3 revealed the seriousness of his spirituality as prevalent when he "wakes up and go to sleep because this is the beginning and the end of the day, and God is the first and last thing that comes to mind." Participant # 3 spoke the above statement, his tear ducts began to swell with water and he had to pause for a moment before completing his statement. The most profound movement when asking this question and throughout the whole interview process was the body posture of Participant # 3, which tensed up when he became emotional. The movement of his hands clinched into a fist, as if he was trying to fight back the tears by tensing up his whole body. There were no words spoken by the researcher during this time. When Participant # 3 looked up, the researcher made eye contact and smiled to assure him that it was all right to feel this emotion and he was doing well.

The same response was experienced with Participant # 5. His emotional reaction came in the way of stuttering while expressing his excitement. Participant # 5 did not tense up, but just became emotional through his tears, as if he was happy that someone understood his joy of knowing Christ and embracing his spirituality as much as he did. This question served as a pivotal point in all of the interviews done with the participants. This section solidified that spirituality was needed in everything they accomplished and experienced in their lives. The researcher was able to recognize each participant for where they were in their spirituality, and to additionally recognize that the power behind the African American young adult male in the urban community is not the physicality, but the spirituality.

Give example(s) of when you have used spirituality as a way of coping.	1	2	3	4	5
Through spoken word (poetry)	X				
Through physical activity	X				
Through praying	X	X	X	X	X
Through expressing thanks (gratitude)	X	X	X	X	X
Through times of trials and tribulations		X	X	X	X
Through music					X

Table # 7: Breakdown of Question 7: Give example(s) of when you have used spirituality as a way of coping.

The breakdown in *Table # 7* demonstrated praying, gratitude, and times of trials and tribulations as the leading examples when spirituality was used as a way of coping for the five participants. The examples expressed by the participants confirmed their belief of spirituality, reinforcing their success in fulfilling God's purpose for their life. Through trials and tribulations and praying, all five participants concurred that surrendering to God was the heart of their spirituality. This act of personal surrender by the participants helped them to conclude that the more you realized how much Christ loved you, the easier spirituality became. When it came to gratitude, the five male participants demonstrated that by seeing life's bright side, especially when it came to difficult situations, enhanced their spiritual connection and helped them to reinforce that it was not about them, but the spirit within them.

Thematic Analysis

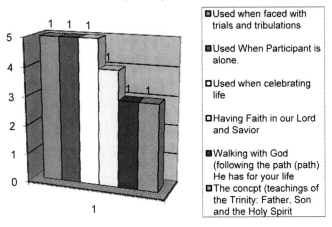

Spirituality-Thematic Analysis

- Used when faced with trials and tribulations
- Used When Participant is alone.
- Used when celebrating life
- Having Faith in our Lord and Savior
- Walking with God (following the path (path) He has for your life
- The concpt (teachings of the Trinity: Father, Son and the Holy Spirit

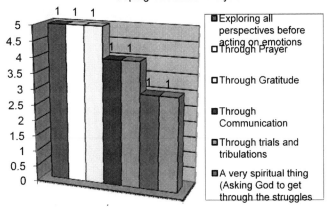

Coping-Thematic Analysis

- Exploring all perspectives before acting on emotions
- Through Prayer
- Through Gratitude
- Through Communication
- Through trials and tribulations
- A very spiritual thing (Asking God to get through the struggles

The transcribed data from the audio taped interviews provided information for the thematic analysis. The phenomenological approach investigated a particular phenomenon that needed to be explained, but for which very little research exists that can provide an effective explanation (Creswell, 2003) Arising themes were presented through reviewed transcribed audiotapes, observation and field notes. It was clear through every participant interviewed that spirituality was the catalyst for their life, and the major coping skills were enhanced as a conduit of spirituality. As mentioned before, the common themes were:

- Christian spirituality was living, depending, humbling and being true to the teachings of Jesus Christ in your daily walk.
- Coping meant dealing with your problems in a positive, Christian way, by asking for help (through God, people, etc.) with the end result having found a way to resolve your problems.
- The main method of coping when it came to anger was exploring all perspectives before acting on emotions.
- The main skill participants had to show spirituality, as a way of coping was through the skill of communication (with God and people).
- Prayer was the source of spirituality in their everyday life.
- Spirituality was felt the most during trials and tribulations, celebrations and quiet times.
- There were always examples of personal lived experiences when using spirituality as a way of coping.

The assumption of phenomenology is to understand the essence of the lived experience without finding a specific basis.

Summary

This chapter offered the data collection and analysis of the research based on the phenomenological approach. Five African-American young adult males from Paterson, New Jersey participated in this study. The premise of the data analysis was based on each participant's interview from lived experiences. Descriptive narratives of each participant were offered. From the data, several themes emerged. Spirituality had a major impact on each participant, especially as a mechanism in coping skills. Embracing spirituality strengthened the lives of these African American young adult males and helped them to overcome the trials and tribulations in life creating a foundation to succeed.

REFERENCES

Bandura, A. (1977). Social Learning Theory. New York: General Learning Press.

Creswell, J.W. (2003). *Research design: Qualitative & quantitative, and mixed methods approaches.* Thousand Oaks, CA: Sage.

Hycner, R. H. (1985). Some guidelines for the phenomenological analysis of interview data. *Human Studies, 8,* 279-303.

McKay, M., Davis, M. & Fanning, P. (1983). How to communicate: The ultimate guide to improving your personal and professional relationships. New York: MJF Books.

Merriam, S.B. (1998). *Qualitative Research and Case Study Applications in Education.* San Francisco, CA; Jossey-Bass.

Moustakas, C. (1994). *Phenomenological research methods.* Thousand Oaks, CA: Sage.

CPSIA information can be obtained at www.ICGtesting.com
Printed in the USA
LVOW11s0828250315

431873LV00001B/39/P